Access to History

General Editor: Keith Randell

The Interregnum 1649-60

Michael Lynch

Hodder & Stoughton

A MEMBER OF THE HODDER HEADLINE GROUP

The cover illustration shows a miniature of Oliver Cromwell (unfinished) by Samuel Cooper (Courtesy of Private Collection/Bridgeman Art Library).

British Library Cataloguing in Publication Data

A catalogue for this book is
available from the British Library

ISBN 0-340-58207-3

First published 1994

Impression number   10 9 8 7 6 5 4 3 2
Year   1998 1997 1996 1995

© 1994 Michael Lynch

Typeset by Sempringham publishing, Bedford
Printed in Great Britain for Hodder & Stoughton Educational, a division of Hodder Headline Plc, 338 Euston Road, London NW1 3BH by Page Bros (Norwich) Ltd

Contents

CHAPTER 1 The Interregnum: an Introduction   1
        1 The English Revolution, 1640-60   1
           a) The Prelude, 1625-40   1
           b) The Breakdown, 1640-2   3
           c) The First Civil War, 1642-6   5
           d) The Failure to reach a Settlement, 1646-9   6
           e) The Trial and Execution of the King, 1649   8
        2 The Interregnum, 1649-60   9
        Study Guides   13

CHAPTER 2 The Rump Parliament, 1649-53   15
        1 Relations between the Rump and the Army   15
        2 The Establishment of the Commonwealth   16
        3 The Rump and the Leveller Threat   17
           a) Background   17
           b) Lilburne and Cromwell   18
           c) Why the Levellers Failed   20
           d) The True Levellers (the Diggers)   22
        4 The Rump and Ireland   22
           a) The Background to the Irish Problem   23
           b) Cromwell in Ireland   24
        5 The Rump and Scotland   28
           a) The Background to the Scottish Crisis   28
           b) Cromwell in Scotland   29
        6 The Record of the Rump   30
           a) Religious Policy   30
           b) Legal and Social Policies   31
           c) Financial Policies   33
        7 The Dissolution of the Rump, April 1653   34
        Study Guides   36

CHAPTER 3 The Search for a Settlement, 1653-8   39
        1 The Nominated Assembly, July-December 1653   39
        2 The Founding of the Protectorate   41
           a) The *Instrument of Government,* December 1653   41
           b) Cromwell's Position as Lord Protector   42
        3 The First Protectorate Parliament, September
              1654-January 1655   43
        4 The Major-Generals, 1655-7   44
        5 The Second Protectorate Parliament, 1656-8   48
           a) The First Session, September 1656-July 1657   48
           b) The *Humble Petition and Advice,* 1657   50

c) The Second Session of Parliament, January-
February 1655   53
6 Cromwell's Last Months   54
Study Guides   54

CHAPTER 4 Cromwell, the Sectaries and the Royalists   58
1 The Radical Sectaries   58
a) Baptists   59
b) Congregationalists (Independents)   60
c) Fifth Monarchists   60
d) Muggletonians   61
e) Seekers and Ranters   61
f) Quakers   62
2 Cromwell and the Sects   63
3 Cromwell and the Royalists   66
4 Cromwell as Protector   68
Study Guides   70

CHAPTER 5 Foreign Policy During the Interregnum   74
1 Background   74
2 The Commonwealth and External Affairs   75
a) The Navigation Act, 1651   76
b) The Dutch War, 1652-4   76
3 Foreign Policy under the Protectorate   77
a) The End of the Dutch War   77
b) The Western Design and War against Spain   78
c) Reactions to the Western Design   81
d) Cromwell's Colonial Policy   81
e) Relations with France   83
f) The Baltic Question   85
4 The Debate on Cromwellian Foreign Policy   85
5 How Successful was Protectorate Foreign Policy?   87
Study Guides   88

CHAPTER 6 The Path to Restoration, 1658-60   91
1 The Protectorate under Richard Cromwell,
September 1658-April 1659   91
a) The Third Protectorate Parliament, January-April
1659   93
2 The Restored Commonwealth, May 1659-February
1660   94
a) The Rump Recalled, May-October 1659   94
b) The Committee of Safety, October-December
1659   96
c) The Recalled Rump, December 1659-February
1660   98
3 The Restored Long Parliament, February-March
1660   99

4 The Convention Parliament, April-May 1660   100
5 The Restoration of Monarchy, May 1660   100
6 Reasons for the Failure of the Republic   102
   a) The Political Weakness of the Republic   102
   b) The Unpopularity of Army Rule   103
   c) The Contribution of Monk   103
   d) Divisions within the Army   103
   e) The Attraction of Monarchy   104
Study Guides   104

CHAPTER 7 Conclusion: The Interregnum in Perspective   109
Study Guides   113

Chronological Table   114

Glossary   116

Further Reading   118

Index   120

Preface

To the general reader

Although the *Access to History* series has been designed with the needs of students studying the subject at higher examination levels very much in mind, it also has a great deal to offer the general reader. The main body of the text (i.e. ignoring the Study Guides at the ends of chapters) forms a readable and yet stimulating survey of a coherent topic as studied by historians. However, each author's aim has not merely been to provide a clear explanation of what happened in the past (to interest and inform): it has also been assumed that most readers wish to be stimulated into thinking further about the topic and to form opinions of their own about the significance of the events that are described and discussed (to be challenged). Thus, although no prior knowledge of the topic is expected on the reader's part, she or he is treated as an intelligent and thinking person throughout. The author tends to share ideas and possibilities with the reader, rather than passing on numbers of so-called 'historical truths'.

To the student reader

There are many ways in which the series can be used by students studying History at a higher level. It will, therefore, be worthwhile thinking about your own study strategy before you start your work on this book. Obviously, your strategy will vary depending on the aim you have in mind, and the time for study that is available to you.

If, for example, you want to acquire a general overview of the topic in the shortest possible time, the following approach will probably be the most effective:

1 Read chapter 1 and think about its contents.
2 Read the 'Making notes' section at the end of chapter 2 and decide whether it is necessary for you to read this chapter.
3 If it is, read the chapter, stopping at each heading to note down the main points that have been made.
4 Repeat stage 2 (and stage 3 where appropriate) for all the other chapters.

If, however, your aim is to gain a thorough grasp of the topic, taking however much time is necessary to do so, you may benefit from carrying out the same procedure with each chapter, as follows:

1 Read the chapter as fast as you can, and preferably at one sitting.
2 Study the flow diagram at the end of the chapter, ensuring that you understand the general 'shape' of what you have just read.

3 Read the 'Making notes' section (and the 'Answering essay questions' section, if there is one) and decide what further work you need to do on the chapter. In particularly important sections of the book, this will involve reading the chapter a second time and stopping at each heading to think about (and to write a summary of) what you have just read.
4 Attempt the 'Source-based questions' section. It will sometimes be sufficient to think through your answers, but additional understanding will often be gained by forcing yourself to write them down.

When you have finished the main chapters of the book, study the 'Further Reading' section and decide what additional reading (if any) you will do on the topic.

This book has been designed to help make your studies both enjoyable and successful. If you can think of ways in which this could have been done more effectively, please write to tell me. In the meantime, I hope that you will gain greatly from your study of History.

Keith Randell

Acknowledgements

The Publishers would like to thank the following for permission to reproduce illustrations in this volume: Miniature of Oliver Cromwell (unfinished) by Samuel Cooper, Private Collection/Bridgeman Art Library, London - cover; The Mansell Collection p. 8; The British Library p. 19; The Cromwell Museum p. 48, p. 52; Guildhall Library, Corporation of London p. 82.

The Publishers would also like to thank the following for permission to reproduce copyright material: Longman Group UK for the extract from B. Coward, *Oliver Cromwell* (1991).

Every effort has been made to trace and acknowledge ownership of copyright. The Publishers will be glad to make suitable arrangements with any copyright holders whom it has not been possible to contact.

CHAPTER 1

The Interregnum: an Introduction

It is helpful to think of the Interregnum as forming the second half of the English Revolution of 1640-60. It covers the years between the execution of Charles I in 1649 and the restoration of his son, Charles II, in 1660. The Interregnum is not to be thought of as a self-contained period. It cannot be understood except by reference to what went before it. It was a set of reactions to the remarkable events of the preceding nine years. We need to begin, therefore, by surveying the major developments of those years and by noting how historians have interpreted them.

A lively controversy exists over when the English Revolution actually began. For the purposes of this introduction, it is appropriate to take the date as 1637. It was in that year that the royal government of Charles I attempted to impose the Anglican Prayer Book upon Scotland. The Scots, large numbers of whom were Presbyterians who objected to having their form of worship dictated to them by an English State Church, rebelled. The rebellion was so serious that an English army had to be raised in an attempt to suppress it. Armies are expensive. The so-called Bishops' Wars of 1637-40 obliged Charles I to recall parliament in 1640 in order to ask it to grant him special subsidies to meet the cost of maintaining the English forces. To understand why the recall of parliament was so significant it is necessary to glance back to the beginning of the reign of Charles I.

1 The English Revolution, 1640-60

a) The Prelude, 1625-40

Charles I, who had become king in 1625, had been angered during the earlier years of his reign by parliament's criticism of his foreign, religious and financial policies. After 1629 he deliberately avoided summoning parliament. During the following 11 years his royal government tried to develop a method of revenue-raising that would end the necessity of calling upon parliament for finance. The royal prerogative was invoked to impose heavy taxation and high customs levies, a deeply unpopular policy with the propertied and merchant classes. The most notorious measure was the raising of ship money, a use of the ancient right of the monarch to levy taxes from the maritime counties for the maintenance of the navy in wartime. Ship money became particularly resented since it was now levied in peacetime and was extended to include the inland counties.

The weakness of Charles's financial measures was that they could work only in peacetime when expenditure could be kept within bounds;

they could not meet extraordinary demands on revenue. Thus the outbreak of a costly war in Scotland in 1637 dramatically changed the situation.

Matters were greatly affected by the issue of religion. Since the Reformation a century earlier, which had involved the rejection of Papal authority in England, the Anglican (English) Church had developed as a broadly Protestant body. By Charles I's time two main strands were identifiable within it, Puritanism and Arminianism. Puritanism had no exact definition. It referred broadly to those Protestants who detested Popery (Roman Catholicism) and were suspicious of a church structure that contained bishops and priests and that demanded uniformity of worship. Puritans also frowned upon the trappings of religious worship. They disliked elaborate ritual and ceremony, believing that these interposed themselves between God and his people. It is important to remember that, up to the period of conflict with which this book deals, Puritanism was not a separate denomination; it was contained within the Anglican Church.

Arminianism, which was the major influence among the bishops and higher clergy of the Church, laid emphasis upon hierarchy, the notion of an ascending order of authority within the Church, with obedience owed by the laity to the parish clergy, by the clergy to the bishops, by the bishops to the archbishops. It stressed the importance of the sacraments and the ritual of worship. Arminianism became the policy of the Church under William Laud, Archbishop of Canterbury from 1633. Laud was a loyal servant of the Crown who believed it was his duty to impose religious conformity and obedience. The zeal with which he pursued this aim was one of the main causes of the royal government's unpopularity during this period of the so-called 'eleven-year tyranny'. Using the Church courts and the prerogative courts, (those which stood outside the common law of the realm and depended on the king's authority for their power), Laud harried those who would not conform. The imposition of the Prayer Book, which laid down detailed regulations about the way in which public worship was to be conducted, was part of his programme for enforcing conformity.

Laud's name is indelibly associated with that of Thomas Wentworth, Earl of Strafford. What Laud was to religion, Strafford was to civil government. As the king's chief minister in the later 1630s, Strafford conducted a policy of 'thorough', aiming to bring order and strong administration into the exercise of royal government. Laud and Strafford became objects of detestation to those who considered their religious and civil freedom was at risk under their policies.

Despite the terror they aroused, Laud and Strafford were beset by a major difficulty; they were strong men in a weak government. As events were to show, at crucial times they did not receive the backing of the King and court whom they were trying to serve.

b) The Breakdown, 1640-2

The very act of calling parliament in April 1640 was evidence of the King's desperate financial plight. This encouraged parliament to go on the offensive. It refused to vote grants or supplies until its grievances over religion and taxation had been dealt with to its satisfaction. Angrily the King dissolved this parliament (later known as the Short Parliament) after only four weeks. But this merely made matters worse for Charles since he now had no means of raising the extra income he desperately needed. In the autumn the failures of the English army in Scotland obliged Charles to summon a new parliament. The scene appeared set for confrontation.

However, modern scholarship has shown that at many points in the crises of 1640 matters might have been prevented from deteriorating had tact and foresight been shown by those involved. One example may be quoted here: the high-handed way in which the Privy Council (roughly equivalent to the modern Cabinet) negotiated with the parliamentary leaders over money supply prevented a workable compromise being reached. It is noteworthy that the Commons' assault on the royal policy was never directed at Charles himself. Members of Parliament were always careful to direct their attack at the corrupt ministers who had misled their monarch. This was not simply a formula for avoiding the taint of treason; it indicated that in no sense was the opposition to royal policy a challenge to monarchy itself. Charles I's majesty was not questioned. The changes that were being demanded were all thought of as falling within the existing constitutional structure. There was nothing revolutionary in intent in what the Commons did, although this is not to deny that it would be revolutionary in effect.

The Long Parliament (as it was to become known) met in an aggressive mood in November 1640. Its members believed that they had the government on the defensive. Led by John Pym, a staunch Presbyterian and a skilful parliamentary manager, the Commons organised themselves to attack the royal policy and assert the role of parliament as an essential part of the constitution. Shrewdly, Pym took as his first objective the bringing down of Strafford. He reasoned that if the chief architect of 'thorough', and by far the most able man in the King's service, could be removed, then the royal policy itself must founder. Strafford was brought before parliament on a charge of high treason. Despite offering a spirited defence, he was condemned and sentenced to death. Now occurred one of the decisive moments in the English Revolution. Would the king defend Strafford, whom he knew to be innocent, or would he sacrifice him as an act of appeasement to parliament? Charles chose the latter course, an act of cowardice and betrayal, as he himself acknowledged at the time of his own execution eight years later.

'Black Tom is dead! Tyranny is dead!', the crowds are reported to have shouted in May 1641 at the news of Strafford's beheading. The way now seemed open for further restrictions to be imposed on the royal power. The King's prerogative courts, Star Chamber and High Commission, were abolished and ship money was declared illegal. Acts were passed, requiring that parliament be called at least once every three years, and outlawing its dissolution except by its own consent. In something of a daze, Charles, who had withdrawn to Scotland in May, gave his assent to all these measures, thus making them constitutional. This was an obvious success for parliament, but it did not diminish the fear among parliamentarians that all their gains might be swept away should the king choose to use his royal authority to dismiss parliament by force of arms. There were constant rumours that this was Charles' intention.

Matters took a new turn in October 1641 with the outbreak of rebellion in Ireland (see page 23). Parliament's greatest anxiety was that if an army were to be raised to put down the Irish rebellion, it might first be used against them. The response of the Commons was to issue the 'Grand Remonstrance', which listed all their political and religious grievances and contained the demand that parliament should appoint the king's ministers. The Remonstrance went too far for many MPs and caused a serious split in parliament. The vote on it was carried by only 11 votes in the Commons and was not considered at all by the Lords. Parliamentary unanimity had obviously broken down. Those who had previously been willing to see the limitation of royal power were now unhappy about the extreme steps that parliament was contemplating. It was from this division that the two sides in the civil war - royalist and parliamentarian - would develop.

Religion was of critical importance in deepening the divide in parliament. Those who believed that the Laudian repression and the Irish rebellion were part of a conspiracy to overthrow the Anglican Church and impose Popery in England looked to parliament for protection. But many of those who earlier had been pleased to see restrictions placed on Laudianism now felt that things were being pushed too far. They began to show concern that the Puritan anti-Laudians were beginning to use parliament as the means of undermining the Anglican Church itself. This had first been apparent in the 'Root and Branch Petition' of the autumn of 1640 which had attacked the episcopal system, and in the subsequent attempt of some parliamentarians to exclude the bishops from the House of Lords.

Charles I returned to London in November 1641, hoping to exploit the divisions appearing in parliament. In a move to keep the initiative, the opposition faction in the Commons proposed impeaching the Queen, Henrietta Maria, on the grounds that she was plotting with the Irish rebels. Outraged by this charge, Charles decided on a show of force. In January 1642 he went in person with his guards to the Commons to arrest the five ringleaders in the impeachment proceedings. However, the five had been forewarned of the king's coming and by the time he arrived at Westminster, they had been smuggled to safety. Charles had to withdraw empty-handed, amid angry members' cries of 'privilege!'.

Charles came very badly out of this incident. He had failed to arrest the five members but at the same time had increased the fears of parliament that he was prepared to use force to overthrow them. The London mob was encouraged to demonstrate in favour of parliament. In fear for his royal dignity and his family's safety, Charles hurriedly left London to return to Scotland. On his journey north he appealed to loyal subjects to rally to him.

Whether war was unavoidable at this point is still a major debating point, but certainly the two sides, as they may now be called, began to prepare for war. In March 1642 parliament drew up a militia ordinance, giving it the right to levy troops. The king countered in June by issuing commissions of array empowering his officials in the counties to raise forces. It was also in June that the Commons delivered to the king the Nineteen Propositions, demanding that he yield a whole range of powers to parliament. The king's reply drafted in June showed that he was not willing to go beyond the concessions he had granted in 1641. In August 1642, Charles raised his standard at Nottingham; the civil war had begun.

c) The First Civil War, 1642-6

It is still usual to refer to the civil war as a struggle between king and parliament, but it has to be remembered that these terms are a form of shorthand. They are imprecise. Approximately one third of the Commons supported the king in the war and two thirds supported parliament. In the House of Lords the proportions were reversed; two thirds supported the king and one third supported parliament. Thus as a body, parliament was split diagonally in half. There was a similar division of support in the country at large; a rough line of demarcation ran from the north-east to the south-west, with parliament stronger to the south of that line and the royalists stronger to the north. This was by no means an exact division; there were pockets of resistance of a royalist or parliamentarian kind dotted throughout enemy territory.

The royalists had the better of the early stages of the war. This was in part due to the reluctance of the aristocratic leaders of the parliamentary forces, the Earl of Essex and the Earl of Manchester, to wage all-out war. It was the reaction against this diffidence that brought Oliver Cromwell to the fore. From his base in East Anglia, Cromwell, hitherto a backbench MP, organised a force which eventually grew into the New Model Army, disciplined, determined, and infused with religious zeal. Those parliamentarians who were determined to achieve complete victory over the king induced the fainter-hearted commanders to surrender their commissions. This was done by a ruse known as the Self-Denying Ordinance (1645), a Commons resolution requiring serving officers to resign their positions and then seek re-appointment. The faint-hearts found that their commissions were not renewed, their places being taken by the fully-committed generals. Cromwell's New Model Army now became increasingly significant, politically as well as militarily, as the war went on.

Wars often have the effect of pushing the combatants in directions that they had not originally planned to go. This was the case with the English civil war. In order to gain military help the English parliament entered into the Solemn League and Covenant with the Scottish Presbyterians in 1643. In return for military support, parliament promised to adopt Presbyterianism as the official religion of England. This was a highly significant development; parliament in its anxiety to defeat the king had now formally committed itself to replacing one form of state religion, Anglicanism, with another, Presbyterianism. This was seen as a betrayal by those parliamentarians who had taken up arms against the king in order to be free of an established church.

The signing of the Solemn League and Covenant also caused a major shift in the relations between parliament and the army, and marked an important stage in emergence of the latter as a political and religious force. As the war progressed, the parliamentary army came increasingly to represent the Protestant sects who wanted freedom of worship for individual congregations without control from a centralised state church. This development ran counter to the trend in the Commons. There, as the signing of the Solemn League and Covenant showed, the upper hand had been gained by those MPs who wanted the replacement of the Laudian Anglican Church with the Presbyterian state model. A critical divergence of attitude had begun to develop between parliament and its own army.

By 1646 parliament's greater economic resources and its control of the major ports including London, the nation's administrative and financial capital, had brought it victory. Militarily, the extraordinary abilities of Oliver Cromwell, who had not taken up arms until he was over forty, proved the major factor in the defeat of Charles's armies, which, whatever the brilliance of their individual commanders, could not match the New Model in organisation, discipline and resolution.

d) The Failure to reach a Settlement, 1646-9

In many ways, the defeat of the king left the situation more uncertain than when war had broken out. Parliament was now divided between the Presbyterians and the 'Independents', the spokesmen of the Protestant sects. The Presbyterian element in the Commons pressed for the disbanding of the army as soon as hostilities were over, but the rank and file soldiers in the infantry and cavalry, supported by their officers, refused to do so until their arrears of pay had been met and they had been indemnified against future prosecution for deeds done during the war. In 1647 the army marched on London in a show of force.

It was the attitude of Charles I that prevented a lasting political settlement from being found after the war ended in 1646. His defeat had not destroyed kingship. He believed he had suffered nothing more than a military reverse. Between 1646 and 1648 Charles entered into negotiations with all the major groups - parliament, army and the Scots - with a view to restoring his authority. He played the groups off against each other and made contradictory promises that he had no intention of keeping. That was why all attempts to find 'an accommodation with his Majesty' eventually broke down. One of Charles's promises led directly to the outbreak of the second civil war in 1648. Late in 1647, the king entered into an 'Engagement' with the Scots in which he promised to do what the English parliament had reneged upon, to adopt Presbyterianism as the official form of church worship. This was almost a complete reversal of the alignment of 1642. Whereas the first civil war had been parliament and Scots against the king, the second civil war was king and Scots against parliament.

In the struggle that followed, the lack of co-ordination between the Scots and the English royalists and the speed at which the army under Fairfax and Cromwell responded rendered Charles I's cause a hopeless one militarily. The crushing defeat of the royalists reinforced a powerful feeling among the army and some of the MPs that Charles I was personally responsible for the further bloodshed and misery of the kingdom. The General Council of the Army, deciding that further negotiations with him were pointless, resolved that he must be removed; not however, 'in a hole and corner manner' but by putting him on public trial. The army wished to clothe its actions in legal form. Modern historians, notably Gerald Aylmer, have made much of this as an illustration of how far the army was from contemplating revolution.

To prepare the way for the trial the General Council decided that the Commons must be cleared of those MPs likely to oppose the plan for bringing the king to account. Accordingly, in December 1648, Colonel Pride, acting on behalf of the Army Council, forcibly debarred from entry to the Commons those MPs, largely Presbyterians, who were intent on continuing discussions with the king. This event has became known as 'Pride's Purge'. Those MPs who remained in the Commons after the Purge were referred to later as the Rump.

Yet again circumstances had forced people of influence into making decisions and taking steps that they would not have contemplated earlier. The climax of this came with the trial and execution of the king in January 1649. Although it was to be dressed in legal forms and justified by arguments of principle, the king's execution marked the culmination of ten years of political failure.

e) The Trial and Execution of the King, 1649

To give themselves the authority to try the king, the Commons asserted early in January 1649 that 'the supreme power in this nation' was now vested solely in them, without the need of king or House of Peers. At the trial, the High Court, specially created by the Rump to prosecute the king, claimed to represent the will of the 'the people of England', against whom the king had offended. This claim, which flew in the face of all precedent and law, was the Rump's weakest point. When the charge was read out, impeaching the king in the name 'of the people of England', a woman in the gallery cried out: 'No, nor the hundredth part of them'. That she was rumoured to be Lady Fairfax, the wife of the commander of parliament's army, showed how deeply the trial of the king had divided the nation.

The trial was in no sense a disinterested attempt to establish Charles' guilt or innocence. It was a show trial; his guilt was assumed from the beginning. It had been expressed at the outbreak of the second civil war in May 1648 when the army had declared its intention 'to call Charles Stuart, that man of blood, to an account for the blood he had shed'.

Contrary to expectation, Charles conducted himself well at his trial. He behaved with dignity and lost the stammer that had habitually handicapped his public speaking. He refused to recognise the court or to plead, but took the opportunity, when permitted to speak, to ask his accusers by what legal authority they brought him before them. It was the one question to which they had no legitimate answer. He had a case grounded in law and tradition that the hastily-created High Court could not match. He rejected the whole proceedings on the grounds that 'a king cannot be tried by any superior jurisdiction on earth'.

Whatever Charles's personal responsibility may have been for the

Charles I's death warrant

civil wars, there is no doubt that he had the better of the argument at his trial. However, his fate was pre-determined. He was declared guilty, condemned to death, and duly beheaded on 30 January 1649.

The next logical step was for the Rump to abolish both the monarchy and the Lords. This was formally done in March 1649, but only after considerable debate about whether it was the right course. The delay and uncertainty suggests how far from being truly revolutionary the Rump actually was. Of course, in one sense there are few things more revolutionary than the beheading of a reigning monarch, but it has to be re-emphasised that Charles's execution was not undertaken primarily in order to bring about a constitutional change. It was foremost a remedy for the insoluble problem of what to do with a defeated king who would not accept his defeat. Republicanism had never been very strong in England. The civil wars had been fought not to destroy kingship but to limit its powers. The decision to try Charles and put him to death was made very late in the struggle between king and parliament. It was an act of desperation that arose from the impossibility of negotiating with him. The members of the purged parliament and of the army who voted for the king's trial and execution considered that there was no alternative to his permanent removal.

The majority of the people in Britain were shocked by the affront to tradition that the execution of an anointed monarch represented. The strength of this feeling is shown by the large number of Charles's opponents who, no matter how much they blamed him for the nation's sufferings, could not bring themselves to be involved in his judicial murder. However, for the regicides (those who signed his death warrant) it was a duty they had to fulfil. Charles was a man 'against whom the Lord himself hath witnessed'. Cromwell is reputed to have said at the time that 'we will cut off his head with the crown upon it' and that the execution was a 'cruel necessity'. There is no hard evidence that he said either of these things, but their sentiment does accurately express the attitude of the regicides in 1649.

2 The Interregnum, 1649-60

These 11 years were taken up with a continual effort to establish a stable constitution to replace the system of monarchy that had been abolished in 1649. Between 1649 and 1653, England was a Commonwealth, ruled by a Council of State appointed by parliament, which was itself the truncated remnant of the Long Parliament first called in 1640. In 1653 Oliver Cromwell, the head of the army, forcibly dissolved this 'Rump' parliament. This was soon followed by the establishment of a Protectorate with Cromwell as Lord Protector, a position he held until his death five years later in 1658. In one obvious sense Cromwell was a military dictator, but this was not his intention. He experimented with various forms of parliament, always with the intention of returning

England to civilian government. The dilemma which he was never able to resolve was that whatever form of constitution was adopted its security could be guaranteed only by the support of the military. At his death in 1658 the army still held the key to any settlement. This was shown when, after two years of political confusion which included the unsuccessful attempt of Cromwell's son, Richard, to carry on the Protectorate, the army played the central role in bringing about the restoration of the Stuart monarchy.

The Interregnum may be characterised, therefore, as a time when those in power sought to establish a form of government which possessed the stability and acceptability of the pre-1640 political system. When this proved impossible to achieve, the various experiments having failed to create the desired constitutional balance, the only logical course was a return to kingship, which, with all its previous shortcomings, was deemed superior to any of the attempts to replace it. But it must be remembered that this description simplifies what was a much more complex process. It does not explain, for example, the existence of the radical social and religious movements of the period. Nonetheless, it does remain a useful broad frame of reference by which to begin analysing the Interregnum.

For a number of decades after the Second World War, the Marxist view of history dominated the interpretations of the English Revolution. There was a strong tendency to view the events of 1640-60 as a class struggle, in which economic considerations pre-determined how the political situation would develop. The crises and conflicts that produced the civil war could only be properly understood if they were set in the broader pattern of social and economic change. The leading representative of this approach was Christopher Hill, acknowledged by all scholars, whatever their own leanings, as a major authority on the English Revolution.

During the last 20 years, studies of the period have been strongly influenced by the revisionist school of historians. Its main thrust has been to dismiss the concept of class-conflict as the major dynamic behind events and to suggest instead that the struggle is better understood as the product of political failure. Many modern scholars, of whom Conrad Russell and Derek Hirst are outstanding examples, emphasise that the struggle between king and parliament was largely brought about by political mistakes and personal errors. They do not deny that there were long-term causes of the troubles, but they argue that these did not make a struggle inevitable. They suggest that if Charles I had been of a different temperament or if he had shown greater political skills, the civil wars and all that followed might have been avoided. This is a corrective to the view that the English Revolution was the climax of a century of social and economic developments that led inexorably to a final struggle for power.

The revisionists warn against reading history backwards or being too impressed by the radical ideas of the time as if these anticipated such later notions as socialism, popular sovereignty and parliamentary democracy. Revisionism emphasises the predominantly conservative aims of those involved in the events of the period; it was a revolution without revolutionaries. According to this interpretation, the period 1640-9 saw individuals and groups being forced by circumstances into going further than they had originally intended. The following period, 1649-60, then witnessed a succession of attempts to make the new situation work. This ultimately failed because those who held power were unable to reconcile the new political and religious order with their own innate conservatism. They then judged that the only way to ensure the stability and security, which had been their objectives in taking up arms against the king in the first place, was by a return to monarchy.

Another important feature of current historiography is the weight given to Irish and Scottish affairs. Historians are now anxious that England should not be considered in isolation; it was one part of the three kingdoms over which the Stuarts ruled. Ronald Hutton has reminded us that we should consider Britain as a whole when we examine the so-called English Revolution. He was careful to call his book on the Interregnum, *The British Republic 1649-60*, for it was during the years of the republic that Ireland and Scotland were politically subjugated to England, producing a situation that has largely determined the character of Britain from that time to the present.

A further consideration of note is that most books generalise when they describe the developments within this period. They tend to concentrate on central and national developments rather than on what was happening locally. This is not a failing. It is in some ways unavoidable. Writers do not have unlimited space; unless they generalise, they cannot give a broad picture or unravel complicated affairs. However, we do need to be reminded that for every general statement that is made, there are probably many exceptions. This observation is particularly relevant to the history of the local communities in this period. The pioneering studies of Alan Everitt into local history have been carried on by teams of scholars whose researches have led to important shifts of emphasis and interpretation of the period overall. John Morrill, Ronald Hutton and David Underdown have all made important contributions in this area.

The figure of Oliver Cromwell overshadows the whole of the Interregnum and he continues to fascinate the observer. Whether this God-obsessed man and peerless general was genuinely seeking the spiritual regeneration of the nation through religious reformation or whether he was a calculating politician intent on gaining and holding personal power are questions over which scholars and biographers continue to disagree. For centuries after his death it was common for him to be regarded as a 'brave bad man', the description given him by the contemporary royalist chronicler, the Earl of Clarendon. Few historians now would be so confident in their definitions. What attracts their attention is the intriguing personal psychology that shaped Cromwell's religious and political outlook and motivated his actions.

Remarkable though Cromwell was, it may well be that his role during the Interregnum has been exaggerated in the past. Recent research has indicated that the Protectorate governments never exercised the degree of centralised control often ascribed to them. Barry Coward, Cromwell's most recent major biographer, has supported those local historians who have pointed out that many of the administrative policies pursued in the 1650s were initiated and shaped at local not national level.

The Interregnum is very much a paradox. Between 1649 and 1660 a series of successive regimes, which owed their existence to a revolution but which in character and attitude were overwhelmingly conservative, sought to restore a stable, traditional, constitution. This creates a danger that the Restoration of 1660 will be seen as having been inevitable and the period from 1649-60 as simply a series of expedients and failed experiments that led step by step to the return of monarchy. Inevitability is a dangerous concept, which historians are reluctant to apply to the events they study. Moreover, even if it were the case that the restoration was unavoidable it would still be important to discover why this was so.

There are a number of features of the Interregnum that have proved of long-term historical significance. John Morrill has gone as far as to claim that, 'we are the product of a history which has left a residue of the traumas of the 1650s in our national psyche'. In the 1650s Scotland and Ireland were brought directly under English rule, making it possible for the first time to speak of 'Britain' as a political entity. Never before had the nation experienced the commanding presence of a standing army in peace time. At no point had England's reputation as a military power stood so high abroad. For the only time in its history, England tried to govern and administer itself with a single chamber parliament, without a monarch, and by reference to a written constitution. It is true that this experiment was presided over for the greater part of the time by a Protector whose authority rested on his military power, but this serves to re-emphasise the extraordinary character of the period and also to explain the interest that it holds for historians.

What modern analysts increasingly stress is that the real historical importance of the Interregnum is to be found in its negative aspects. The lesson of the period was that, despite valiant efforts to prove the contrary, the only workable alternative to monarchy was rule by the military. It was an alternative that very few wanted. Writing in 1992, David L.Smith, one of the younger historians of the Interregnum, remarked

The years 1649-60 still mark an aberration in English constitu-tional history . . . Yet it is precisely this fact which makes the

Interregnum so important. Its long-term significance lies not in what it created but in what it *discredited*.

Making Notes on the 'Introduction'

Your aim following the reading of this chapter should be to make certain i) that you have understood the principal features of the English Revolution of 1637-60, and ii) that you are aware of the key issues and arguments relating to it. Try to write brief answers to the following questions. This will reveal whether or not you have grasped the important points.

1 What were the main developments in English history in the period 1637-49?
2 Why it is appropriate to regard the Interregnum as a commentary on the failures of the English Revolution?
3 In what ways have revisionist historians redefined the English Revolution and the Interregnum?

Studying 'The Interregnum'

No historical period can be fully understood without reference to the time that preceded it. This is especially true of the Interregnum, since it was in all essential respects a reaction to what had occurred between 1637 and 1649, the period of the English Revolution. It is important, therefore, when studying the Interregnum to be aware of the main political, religious and military developments that constituted the Revolution. An important aid to that awareness is a knowledge of terminology. Words in the seventeenth century often have shades of meaning that they do not carry in modern usage. It is religious terms that often cause the most difficulty since they relate to a set of concepts that are often foreign to the modern student. It would be worthwhile making a conscious effort to gain an understanding of key terms by using the definitions within the text and in the Glossary.

Cromwell is the outstanding figure of the Commonwealth and Protectorate. He remains an individual of enduring fascination for the historian. New biographies which modify our understanding of him appear regularly. While examiners do not require candidates to be entirely up-to-date, they do justifiably expect them to know that interpretations of Cromwell change. References to Oliver Cromwell are to be found throughout this book and Chapter 4 contains an assessment of his role in the Interregnum. It is possible for those concerned solely with studying Cromwell as Lord Protector to use this chapter as an introduction to some of the key features of his Protectorate. But students wanting a fuller coverage need to examine him against the background of his times as set out in the other chapters, particularly numbers 2, 3 and 7.

This book concentrates largely on domestic issues, but readers seeking a broader perspective are encouraged to consult Chapter 5, which deals with foreign affairs during the Interregnum. It should also be pointed out that to gain a complete picture of Cromwell students need to study his conduct of foreign policy, an area that provides vital insights into his attitudes and beliefs.

One of the attractions of the Interregnum as a period of study is that it can be broken down logically into neat compartments, such as 'Commonwealth', 'Protectorate', 'foreign policy', 'Cromwell', and 'Restoration'. These obviously overlap and interconnect at many points, but it is possible to study each of them as a distinct topic. That is the approach followed in this book.

At all levels of historical study considerable attention is now being directed towards an understanding of historiography - the writing and interpretation of history. The period of English history covered by this book is an especially rich one for historiographical analysis. Chapters 1, 4, and 7, offer a number of direction-finders in this area of study.

the Prelude - the English Revolution, 1640-9

'thorough' and the '11-year tyranny' - Laud and Strafford, 1629-40
King and Parliament, 1640-2
the first civil war 1642-6
Solemn League and Covenant, 1643
Cromwell and the New Model Army
the royalists defeated, 1646
failure to reach 'an accommodation with His Majesty', 1646-8
the Leveller movement, 1647
the second civil war, 1648
royalists again defeated, 1648
Pride's Purge, 1648
the trial and execution of the King, 1649

the Interregnum

the Commonwealth, 1649-53
the Protectorate of Oliver Cromwell, 1653-8
the Protectorate of Richard Cromwell, 1658-9
the path to Restoration, 1659-60

aspects of historiography

Summary - The Interregnum: an Introduction

CHAPTER 2

The Rump Parliament, 1649-53

1 Relations between the Rump and the Army

Colonel Pride had carried out his purge of the Long Parliament in December 1648 on the orders of the General Council of the Army. This Council had no constitutional authority, but circumstances had undeniably made it a formidable political force. It was well represented in parliament since a large number of the army officers were also MPs, Oliver Cromwell being a notable example. The plain fact was that it had been the army that had brought the Rump into being. 'What it can do, it can undo'. If the Council chose to insist upon a certain policy or course of action, it would be difficult for the Rump to resist it, let alone ignore it. Thus, although in theory the army after 1648 continued as the servant of parliament, in reality the relationship had been reversed.

Both Thomas Fairfax (Lord General of the Army) and Oliver Cromwell (Lieutenant-General, in charge of the cavalry), had been slow to accept the necessity of the king's trial. Cromwell, far from being the organiser of events, did not return to London until after Pride's Purge had taken place. Indeed, he seems deliberately to have delayed his return in order to avoid having to make a decision. For about three weeks after the purge he appears to have had hopes that a settlement with Charles was still possible. However, as was invariably the case with Cromwell, once he had made up his mind he acted in a totally resolute manner as if no doubts remained. This was an aspect of his belief that it was God who directly guided his judgements.

There is little doubt that by 1649 Oliver Cromwell's outstanding military successes and involvement in the removal of the king had made him a powerful figure. But it is important to emphasise that at this stage he held no constitutional office that conferred power on him. As a soldier he was technically still the servant of parliament, and was subordinate to Lord Fairfax. However, since Fairfax had chosen to withdraw from public affairs, Cromwell became increasingly important politically. His rise to prominence is an example of how in times of uncertainty it is actual rather than theoretical power that matters. Whatever parliamentarians might claim to the contrary, the army was the *de facto* power in the land. As a consequence, Cromwell, the effective leader of the army, became the dominant figure in the nation. Although this did not mean he was all-powerful - he never became that - it did mean that his actions would be a major determinant of how the political situation would develop.

Out of the 470 original members of the House of Commons in the Long Parliament, 211 had survived Pride's Purge. But they were not a united body. No more than 70 of them were involved in the setting up of the High Court that tried the king, and of these only 43 members signed his death warrant. This suggests that Pride's Purge had not reduced parliament to being simply the mouthpiece of the army, and it soon became clear that the Rump was far from regarding itself as dependent on the army for its authority. It claimed to be the legitimate continuation of the Long Parliament first elected in 1640, and therefore, entitled to the loyalty and obedience of the whole nation, including the army. It was a hollow claim. The truth was that the Rump existed as the result of a military purge, a state of affairs that compromised its authority throughout its four years of government.

This is not to suggest that England was under direct military rule after Pride's Purge. Modern historians have emphasised what a remarkably restrained body the army was. Although the radical group, the Levellers, were influential in the ranks after 1647 (see page 18), they were very much a minority and were restricted to certain regiments. The army overall never became radicalised. It was always under the control of the Army Council, the body, which, since the formation of the New Model during the first civil war had been responsible for formulating military policy and exercising authority over the troops. The Army Council was composed of the higher-ranking officers (often referred to as 'Grandees'). They were men of good birth, such as Fairfax, or of property, such as Cromwell, who were certainly not in favour of further political or social upheaval. Indeed, rather than a military takeover, Pride's Purge may be interpreted as an example of the army's moderation in that it wished to retain the essential elements of constitutional government. The Army Council resisted those who urged a total dispersal of the Long Parliament and the appointment of an entirely new legislature.

2 The Establishment of the Commonwealth

Care was taken not to use the word 'republic' to describe England without a king. In the statute of 13 February 1649, which set up a Council of State to act as the government, England was defined as a 'Commonwealth'. This was confirmed in May by an Act declaring England to be a 'Commonwealth and Free State'.

The first Council of State was composed of 41 members, 34 of whom were MPs. Its composition again reflected the conservatism of the Rump. It was successful in preventing a number of influential officers, including Ireton and Thomas Harrison, the leader of the Fifth Monarchists (see page 60), from being voted on to the Council.

It should be stressed that the Rump did not intend the abolition of monarchy and the declaration of a Commonwealth to be the prelude to a revolution. They were meant to consolidate what had been achieved by the defeat of the royalists in the civil wars. The Rump's purpose was to preserve rather than to change the constitution. It was claimed that the king had tried to subvert the fundamental laws of the kingdom and to impose a tyranny. That was why it had been necessary to remove him. As for the House of Lords, the argument was that it had ceased to play its proper constitutional role in that it had made no effort to prevent the royal tyranny. Moreover, its numbers had dwindled to a mere handful, thus making its abolition simply a formal recognition of its obsolescence.

However, not all MPs thought along these lines. Cromwell wondered whether there was not a case for keeping an upper house. He warned the Rump that it would be short-sighted 'to take these courses to incense the peers against them when they had more need to study a near union with them'. His views appear to have been shaped by his wish to preserve good relations with the aristocracy. This again illustrates his lack of revolutionary intent, certainly in social terms. Although he subsequently accepted the abolition of the Lords, Cromwell provided further evidence of his conservative leanings when he persuaded the Rump to substitute a milder oath of loyalty to the new regime for the one originally drafted. The first form of the oath had required those joining the Council of State to recognise the validity of Pride's Purge and the king's execution. Cromwell's compromise version merely asked that the Councillors declare their loyalty to 'the present parliament in the maintenance and defence of the public liberty of the nation'.

This concession eased the way for those who had earlier found themselves unable to approve of the purge and the king's trial. They could now openly accept the new Commonwealth. The result was that the MPs previously excluded by Pride's Purge were able to retake their seats unchallenged and without affront to their consciences. David Underdown has stressed the significance of this: 'by encouraging as many MPs as possible to align themselves with the Commonwealth, even if in their hearts they did not believe in it, the original Rumpers themselves hoped to destroy what impetus the revolution possessed'.

The conservatism of the Rump disappointed and embittered those radicals who had expected Charles I's execution and the creation of the Commonwealth to be followed by a social and religious reformation. The most immediate radical challenge came from the Levellers.

3 The Rump and the Leveller Threat

a) Background

The Leveller movement was one of the most remarkable political developments to grow out of the English Revolution. It had begun in London during the first civil war among the 'middling-sort' of civilians, such as shop-keepers and tradesmen, and soon became influential in a number of army regiments. The basic principle of the Levellers was that sovereignty lay not with parliament but with the people. They demanded the extension of the parliamentary franchise, reform of the legal system, and the recognition of certain fundamental rights, including freedom of worship.

These socially disruptive ideas were unacceptable to the Grandees, the conservative-minded senior army officers. However, between 1647 and 1649 it had served the interests of the Grandees to appear to go along with some of the Leveller demands. This had been done in order to preserve the loyalty of the rank and file during the troubled years of political realignment that led to the second civil war. In 1647 the Grandees had shrewdly incorporated into their plan for a settlement with the king (known as the *Heads of the Proposals*) a number of clauses from the Leveller document, the *Agreement of the People*. This was a matter of expediency; the Grandees had no basic sympathy with Leveller ideas, as had been revealed in the deep disagreements over constitutional rights in the army debates at Putney in 1647 and at Windsor in 1648. Moreover, when Leveller-inspired mutinies had broken out Cromwell had acted immediately to crush them.

b) Lilburne and Cromwell

In December 1648, at the time of Pride's Purge, when the Army Council was anxious to maintain army unity, particularly in London, the Levellers seemed again to be influential. But, as earlier, this proved illusory. The new Commonwealth created in the wake of the king's execution in no respect represented a concession to Leveller demands.

John Lilburne, the leading Leveller, swiftly recognised this. In February 1649 he published a withering attack on the Rump. His main charge was well expressed in the title of his pamphlet, *England's New Chains Discovered*. He denounced the Rump for seizing power from the people and he condemned the Council of State as an unelected clique to whom the people of England owed neither loyalty nor obedience. In another pamphlet, he accused Cromwell of high treason for his part in the king's execution. Such defiance could not be tolerated; Lilburne and three fellow-pamphleteers were arrested and brought before the Council of State, which committed them to the Tower of London.

Lilburne's stand helped to inspire resistance in the ranks of the army. Dislike of the Rump combined with the soldiers' fear of being sent to Ireland, with their arrears unpaid, led to a rash of protests, including the republication of the *Agreement of the People*. In May a number of units mutinied. Cromwell was instructed by the Rump to crush this rising. He needed little prompting. Lilburne in his account of his interrogation by the Council of State recorded Cromwell as saying of the Levellers:

1 I tell you, you have no other way to deal with these men but to break them, or they will break you; yea, and bring all the guilt and blood and treasure shed and spent in this kingdom upon your heads and shoulders, and frustrate and make void all that work

5 that, with so many years' industry, toil and pain you have done, and so render you to all rational men in the world as the most contemptiblest generation of silly, low-spirited men in the earth, to be broken and routed by such a despicable, contemptible generation of men as they are.

Cromwell's severity and the speed with which he moved against the Levellers in 1649 illustrated his determination to win support for the Commonwealth from the traditional governing classes by proving that the new regime would not tolerate social disruption. Having assured the loyal regiments of the Rump's intention to settle their arrears of pay, he appealed for their assistance in subduing 'the army revolters which are now called by the name of Levellers'. Then he and Fairfax chased the retreating Levellers across two counties before cornering them at Burford in Oxfordshire on 14 May. After a token resistance the mutineers surrendered; they were court-martialled, and three of their ringleaders were shot. This, together with the overwhelming of two mutinous troops of cavalry in Northamptonshire two days later, marked the end of the Leveller rising in the army and of the Leveller movement as a political force in the country at large. Lilburne was twice tried for sedition, first in 1649 and again in 1653. He was acquitted on both occasions to great public acclaim. But 'free-born' John was too

AN IMPEACHMENT
OF
HIGH TREASON
AGAINST

Oliver Cromwel, and his Son in Law Henry Ireton Esquires, late Members of the late forcibly dissolved House of Commons, presented to publique view; by Lieutenant Colonel Iohn Lilburn close Prisoner in the Tower of London, for his real, true and zealous affections to the Liberties of his native Country.

In which following Discourse or Impeachment, he engageth upon his life, either upon the principles of Law (by way of indictment, the only and alone legall way of all tryals in England) or upon the principles of Parliaments ancient proceedings, or upon the principles of reason (by pretence of which alone, they lately took away the Kings life) before a legal Magistracy, when there shal be one again in England (which now in the least there is not) to prove the said Oliver Cromwel guilty of the highest Treason that ever was acted in England, and more deserving punishment and death.

Lilburne's impeachment of Cromwell

disruptive a figure to be allowed to go free. He was held in custody in a variety of prisons until his death in 1657.

c) Why the Levellers Failed

The question arises as to why a movement which had seemed so powerful only a short time before should have been so easily crushed. There are several explanations. One is that the Levellers had not been as strong as they first appeared. The extent of Leveller influence, both in the army and in the country as a whole, has tended to be exaggerated by earlier historians. In 1649 the Leveller movement was little more than three years old, far too short a time for it to have taken root in English society. The Leveller leaders, such as Lilburne, Overton and Walwyn, were effective propagandists, and attracted considerable attention. But attention does not necessarily mean support. We now know that the Leveller 'agitators' in the ranks had very limited success. For example, they were never able to persuade more than a small minority of the army units to follow them into open defiance of authority. Out of an army of 40,000 barely 800 soldiers joined the revolt in May 1649. The truth was that although the army rank and file had certainly become politicised since 1647, this was not in terms of radical ideology. The troops were primarily concerned with gaining better pay and conditions of service. When Cromwell and Ireton in 1649 successfully pressed the Rump to provide the backpay owed to the soldiers, unrest in the ranks was greatly reduced.

A second explanation is that by 1649 the conditions which had given the Levellers the limited strength they had possessed had changed. There had been occasions during the previous two years when the uncertainty of the times had encouraged the spread of Leveller ideas. The failure to reach a settlement with the king and the disruption of the second civil war had created an unstable situation, made worse by the economic depression of the late 1640s when poor harvests had led to bread shortages and high prices. Such conditions made Leveller arguments appear attractive as a means of protesting against the grimness of the prevailing conditions. But when better times returned in 1649, in the form of improved harvests, lower prices and higher wages, the Levellers had less fertile ground for sowing dissension.

A still greater restriction on the strength of the Levellers was that they had very few adherents among the officers. Although on occasion the Grandees were prepared to enter into debate with the Levellers, they were unwilling to forego their natural conservatism by actively supporting a group of social radicals. The inability of the Leveller movement to make headway among the officers was of a piece with its failure to gain substantial support in parliament, either before or after Pride's Purge. With the exception of Henry Marten, a committed republican, no major parliamentarian was prepared to sympathise publicly with the Levellers. This failure to win backing among the highest echelons of army and parliament denied the Levellers an effective power base. A similar limitation applied geographically. At no time, outside London and parts of the south-east, did the movement command regular support.

It is also true that the Levellers never really produced a co-ordinated programme of action for changing society. Certainly, the *Agreement of the People* and *England's New Chains Discovered* expressed striking ideas, but these did not amount to a practical alternative constitution. They were essentially outbursts of frustration at the political and social imbalance which allowed, first a royal despotism and then a parliamentary one, to operate in England.

The Levellers' threat to the traditional social balance and order frightened the men of property. The weight of modern research suggests that the upheavals of 1640 onwards were essentially political rather than social. The traditional ruling class remained very much in control. Whatever their differing views on religion and the constitution, the controlling classes invariably closed ranks in the face of a challenge to their customary authority. The Levellers could make little headway against this.

In addition, the Levellers were never numerous enough or sufficiently aggressive to offer a serious threat. They often blustered aggressively, and individuals such as Lilburne were capable of exciting considerable fear, but they were never fully committed to the use of force. Even had they been, there was the awesome figure of Cromwell confronting them. As long as the great body of the army remained loyal to their commanders, there was never a realistic chance that the Levellers could impose themselves by force of arms. As Austin Woolrych put it: 'The Levellers were in fact a precociously well-organized pressure group rather than a revolutionary movement, and much more interested in principles than in power'.

It should be noted that the word 'Leveller' was in many ways misleading. Indeed, much of the pamphlet literature the movement produced was concerned with denying that they intended the levelling of society. Most modern historians now warn against viewing the Levellers as democrats in anything approaching a modern sense. They did not believe in universal suffrage. They wanted the vote for the 'middling sort', by which they meant self-made people as craftsmen, shopkeepers and the smaller property-owners. Their movement never represented the poor and showed no interest in the agricultural labourers. It was almost exclusively an urban movement. In demanding an extended franchise it deliberately excluded wage earners and servants. As a result the Leveller movement fell between two stools. It frightened the propertied classes and so was never able to win support among people of influence. At the same time, it failed to appeal to more than a limited section of the lower orders and so never became a broad-based movement.

d) The True Levellers (the Diggers)

In this context, a broader historiographical point is worth making. The once widely-held view that radicalism was a major force in England at this time has largely been abandoned. There was never a single radical movement. There were various radical groups but these did not come together to form a serious social or political force, still less a threat. They are interesting as precursors of the socialism or liberalism of a later century, but in their own time they did not remotely suggest that they would take power - even had that been their aim. Their influence was minimal.

How far the Levellers were from being a truly revolutionary force is evident from a comparison of them with a movement that made a brief and notorious appearance in 1649. Early in that year, a group of about 50 people, calling themselves the 'True Levellers', took over a patch of wasteland on St.George's Hill in Surrey, which they began to cultivate. This was the practical expression of their belief that land and property belonged not to individuals but to the community. They called for an end of private property. In an exact sense, they were communists. Their inspiration was in large part biblical, but they also looked back to a time before the Norman Conquest when, in their belief, Englishmen had been free because the land had been held in common.

Such a movement was too visionary for its time. It was an intolerable affront to the established rights of property. The inevitable reaction occurred. The Council of State ordered Fairfax to interrogate Gerard Winstanley and William Everard, the two leading 'diggers', as they were jeeringly called. An army unit then supervised the destruction by a local mob of the crops sown on the wasteland. The diggers attempted to carry on with their plan of making 'the earth a common treasury', but local hostility and interference proved too much and the movement collapsed. A similar fate befell the digger colonies that had been set up in ten other southern and midlands counties. At no time did active diggers number more than a few hundred.

4 The Rump and Ireland

When the English Commonwealth was established in 1649 its most immediate task was to subdue rebellion in Ireland and Scotland. Active opposition to the imposition of English authority had been continuous in Scotland since 1637 and in Ireland since 1641. In 1649, having suppressed the royalists at home and executed King Charles I, the new regime now had the opportunity to crush resistance in the other two kingdoms.

a) The Background to the Irish Problem

Ireland was the more immediately pressing of the two problems. Following the execution of Charles I, the Stuarts' chief Irish supporter, the Earl of Ormonde, had been successful in persuading the Protestant royalists in southern Ireland to join with the Catholics in a league against parliament. Charles II, as he had entitled himself immediately on hearing of his father's death, hoped to use Ireland as a base for winning back the Stuart throne. He judged, not unrealistically, that the great mass of the Irish Catholic population had reason to dread the new English Commonwealth. In 1641 the Irish Catholics had risen in a ferocious attack upon the Protestant settlers in Ulster. It was an outburst of pent-up rage at the policy of 'plantation' pursued by English governments since Tudor times and designed to keep the rebellious Irish in order. Plantation involved dispossessing the native Irish of their land and resettling it with English and Scottish settlers, usually of the most extreme Protestant kind. What had deepened bitterness still further had been the severely repressive religious and financial policies imposed on the Irish Catholics by Strafford as Lord Lieutenant of Ireland in the late 1630s.

Such was the savagery of the Irish rising of 1641 that it was pointed to thereafter by English Protestants as the sure proof of the irreversibly evil character of Irish Popery. The English parliament pledged itself to destroy the Irish 'Antichrist', a term denoting particular detestation for creatures whose loathsome behaviour was evidence that they belonged to the damned. The attitude derived from a belief in predestination, one of the fundamental Calvinist doctrines. Strict predestinarians held that human beings fell into one of two groups, the godly, those whom the Almighty had preordained for eternal salvation, and the ungodly, those whom He had preordained for eternal damnation.

Those English parliamentarians who held such beliefs were easily convinced that Charles I's granting of concessions to the Irish Catholics in 1643, a move intended to win them over to his side in the war against parliament, was part of a grand Popish design to subvert the Protestant religion throughout the three kingdoms. In 1643 Nehemiah Wallington, a Puritan leather-worker, had expressed the attitude of his co-religionists when he had declared: 'surely the Lord will not suffer the king nor his posterity to reign but the Lord at last will require blood at their hands'. Wallington likened Charles I to the biblical King Josiah whose idolatries had led to the Babylonish captivity of the Israelites. It was such reasoning that strengthened parliament's resolve both to defeat the king and to punish the Irish. The pre-occupation with the civil wars in England delayed parliament from carrying out this latter pledge, but in 1649 the moment was opportune. From the beginning, therefore, parliament's campaign in Ireland was more than simply a matter of subduing royalist rebels. It was an occasion for wreaking vengeance on an ungodly people.

b) Cromwell in Ireland

Cromwell was appointed Lord Lieutenant in charge of parliament's army in March 1649. After some months' delay, caused by his insistence on assembling adequate supplies, Cromwell landed with 10,000 men in Ireland early in August. In an odd way the delay had worked to his advantage since it had encouraged Ormonde to risk an open attack on the English troops already in Ireland. Ormonde had underestimated the strength of the English force and in an engagement at Rathmines early in August his followers had been surprisingly defeated. The effect of this reverse was to put Ormonde and the royalists on the defensive and to hand Cromwell the initiative even before he arrived in Ireland.

The offensive strategy that Cromwell followed had, therefore, already been conceded to him. As a consequence, his nine-month campaign in Ireland was essentially a matter of advances and sieges of defended positions. Although Ormonde's forces out-numbered the English army, they were no match for it in artillery or discipline. In addition, parliament's control of the Irish Sea meant that Cromwell's army was kept regularly supplied, a luxury which Ormonde's troops never

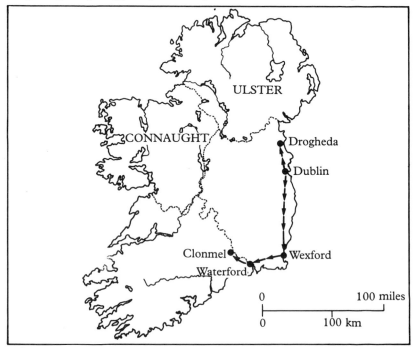

Cromwellian Ireland

enjoyed. It had been Ormonde's hope that Owen Roe O'Neill, the charismatic leader of the Irish peasantry, would bring his forces down from the north to form a royalist combination against Cromwell. However, O'Neill's slowness to respond and then his death in November put an end to such plans. It was, nonetheless, the fear that an alliance between Ormonde and O'Neill might be formed that led Cromwell to begin his campaign with an advance on Drogheda, a fortified town to the north of Dublin that commanded the main north-south route.

Since Cromwell shared the prevailing parliamentarian view of the Irish as deserving special retribution, there was a brutal logic about the exceptional severity with which he treated them. The most notorious examples of his merciless approach are the English army's massacres of the Irish at Drogheda in September 1649 and at Wexford a month later. There is a chilling similarity about the fate that befell both places. Drogheda and Wexford were fortified strongholds in which civilians had gathered as well as troops. Since the towns were judged to be strategically important, military considerations required that they both be taken. In accordance with the rules of war of the time, the occupants were offered quarter if they surrendered. When they refused, Cromwell instructed his troops to kill the inhabitants after the towns had been stormed and captured.

As with most atrocity stories, it is difficult to arrive at the exact truth. There are modern scholars who suggest that the massacres may not have been on so large a scale as has been customarily believed, and that at Drogheda there may well have been no civilian fatalities. But in a sense this line of argument begs the question. It is not the actual numbers or the details that matter. It is the cast of mind that conceives of vengeance as a justifiable policy that gives the Cromwellian campaign in Ireland a particular ferocity. Moreover, the evidence shows that Cromwell himself was very conscious of how far his conduct in Ireland diverged from his own normal standards. His letters describing the events take the form of lengthy justifications for what his army had done. He clearly felt the need to explain, if not to excuse, himself. In his report to parliament describing the storming of Drogheda he wrote:

1 The enemy retreated, divers of them, into the Mill-Mount, a place
   very strong and of difficult access ... Our men getting up to them
   were ordered by me to put them all to the sword. And indeed,
   being in the heat of action, I forbade them to spare any that were in
5 arms in the town ... About one hundred of them possessed
   St.Peter's church-steeple ... These being summoned to yield to
   mercy, refused, whereupon I ordered the steeple of St.Peter's
   Church to be fired, where one of them was heard to say in the
   midst of the flames: 'God damn me, God confound me; I burn, I
10 burn' ... When they submitted, their officers were knocked on the

head and every tenth man of the soldiers killed, and rest shipped for the Barbadoes. I am persuaded that this is a righteous judgement of God upon these barbarous wretches, who have imbrued their hands in so much innocent blood; and that it will
15 tend to prevent the effusion of blood for the future, which are the satisfactory grounds to such actions, which otherwise cannot but work remorse and regret ... It is remarkable that these people, at the first, set up the mass [the central act of Catholic worship] in some places of the town that had been monasteries; but afterwards
20 grew so insolent that, the last Lord's day before the storm, the Protestants were thrust out of the great Church called St.Peter's, and they had public mass there: and in this very place near one thousand of them were put to the sword, fleeing thither for safety. I believe all the friars were knocked on the head.

The taking of Drogheda effectively secured the English army's control of the north of Ireland. With this achieved, Cromwell turned back south and began a long advance that within six months brought the whole of the country under his army's domination. It was during the southern march that the massacre of Wexford occurred. It was a re-run of the horrors of Drogheda, with even greater casualties. Cromwell admitted to a death toll of at least 2,000. In his account to parliament, he again ascribed the massacre to the will of God; it was His fitting punishment on the ungodly.

1 His righteous justice brought a just judgement upon them, causing them to become a prey to the soldier, who in their piracies had made preys of so many families, and made with their bloods to answer the cruelties which they had exercised upon the lives of
5 divers poor Protestants.

Cromwell also added, more revealingly than perhaps he knew, that he and his soldiers had been 'crazed' by the excitement of battle. The religious well-spring of his hatred of Catholic Ireland was clearly evident in a pamphlet published in January 1650 and entitled:

1 A Declaration of the Lord Lieutenant of Ireland, For the Undeceiving of deluded and seduced People: which may be satisfactory to all that do not wilfully shut their eyes against the light. In answer to certain late declarations and Acts, framed by the
5 Irish Popish Prelates and Clergy.

In the course of his ferocious address Cromwell remarked:

1 You, unprovoked put the English to the most unheard of and most barbarous massacre (without respect of sex and age) that ever the sun beheld ... You are part of Antichrist, whose Kingdom the

Scriptures so expressly speaks should be laid in blood; yea in the
5 blood of the Saints. You have shed great store of it already, and ere
it be long, you must all of you have blood to drink; even the dregs
of the cup of the fury and wrath of God, which will be poured unto
you! ... I meddle not with any man's conscience. But if by liberty of
conscience, you mean a liberty to exercise the Mass, I judge it best
10 to use plain dealing, and to let you know, where the Parliament of
England have power, that will not be allowed of.

In his letters from Ireland at this period Cromwell repeatedly claimed
that the severity of his methods would prevent a greater 'effusion of
blood'. Historians are divided on the accuracy of this claim. To cite two
modern authorities by way of example: Ronald Hutton has accepted
Cromwell's contention that his harsh measures did cow the Irish into a
quicker submission, thereby shortening the struggle and saving lives.
Hutton has further suggested that judged by the European standards of
his day Cromwell was not notably severe; he argues with reference to
Ireland that 'to magnify the actions of Cromwell remains a glaring
example of bad history'. A different emphasis has been given by Barry
Coward, a biographer of Cromwell; he has pointed out that in the event
the Drogheda and Wexford massacres did not terrorise the other
garrisons into rapid surrender, and that the towns of Dungarvan,
Waterford and Clonmel fell to Cromwell only after determined and
prolonged resistance. In taking Clonmel in April 1650, the English army
suffered the loss of over 2,000 men.

Whatever difficulties Cromwell may have faced, there is no doubt
that by the time of his recall to England in May 1650 his work was
largely done. The royalist cause in Ireland was a lost one. Henry Ireton
took over as commander of the English forces, but his task, and that of
Charles Fleetwood who succeeded him, was essentially a mopping-up
operation. In completing Cromwell's subjugation of Ireland, Ireton and
Fleetwood took decisions of the the utmost significance for the
immediate and long-term future of Anglo-Irish relations. The previous
plantation policies were continued. To prevent further Irish risings the
lands of the defeated royalists leaders were confiscated and given to
Protestant settlers. Over 40,000 Catholic families were dispossessed. By
1660 Catholic ownership of land was a bare 20 per cent, compared with
60 per cent in 1641. This had the additional effect of further reducing
the condition of the mass of the Catholic peasantry, whose only possible
future was as despised and ill-protected labourers under the new
Protestant landed ascendancy.

This policy was not simply a matter of retribution against the Irish
rebels. The expropriation of land provided a way for the Commonwealth to meet some of its heavy financial commitments. Soldiers were
encouraged to accept land in Ireland in lieu of their arrears of pay. Land
was also offered to the many creditors that parliament had acquired

since 1642. Some historians have even suggested that it was debt rather than religious or political principle that dictated the Commonwealth's policy towards Ireland.

5 The Rump and Scotland

a) The Background to the Scottish Crisis

Scottish resistance to the English parliament was a mixture of nationalism and religion. The Scots had long objected to political dictation from London, whether by king or parliament. They had been especially irked by their subjection to the Anglican Church with its system of interfering bishops and priests. This was why Calvinism was so attractive to the Scots since it involved the ending of Anglicanism and its replacement by a Scottish Presbyterian state church. The Solemn League and Covenant in 1643 (see page 6) had committed the English parliament to introducing this. However, developments within parliament following the defeat of the king in 1646 threatened to destroy Scottish hopes. By the time of the second civil war in 1648, Presbyterian influence in the Long Parliament had been superseded by that of the Independents, the representatives of the Protestant congregations, who objected to exchanging one form of state church for another. Frustrated by this turn of events, the Presbyterians began to consider that an alliance with the king might now be a better way of achieving their original aims.

Charles I sought to take advantage of the divisions in the Protestant ranks. He was quite prepared to compromise his position as head of the Anglican Church by entering into agreement with the Scottish Covenanters. In December 1647 he signed an 'Engagement' with a Presbyterian faction led by the Duke of Hamilton, in which he undertook to adopt Presbyterianism as the state religion in return for military support to enable him to subdue parliament.

Despite the defeat of Charles I in the second civil war, the 'Engagers' remained the dominant influence in Scotland at the time of the king's execution. They immediately proclaimed his son as their lawful monarch. Charles II hoped that this would lead to a full-scale Scottish uprising on his behalf, but the divisions within Scotland between Presbyterians, Episcopalians and Catholics prevented a united front being formed. This was illustrated by the failure of the Earl of Montrose, the Stuarts' most dedicated supporter in Scotland, to mount a serious royalist challenge to the Rump. Nonetheless, Charles persevered. In April 1650 he declared his willingness to enter into agreement with the Scots. Two months later he returned in person to Scotland and formally swore to the Covenant on terms very similar to those his father had accepted in 1647. Charles's willingness to take the Covenant and form an alliance with the Marquess of Argyll, the leading Covenanter, had been quickened by the execution of Montrose in May 1650 at the hands of parliament's representatives in Edinburgh.

b) Cromwell in Scotland

It was the growing Scottish danger that obliged the Rump to recall Cromwell from Ireland in 1650. When Fairfax declined to lead the English army against the Scots, Cromwell was appointed in June to replace him as Lord General and Commander-in-Chief. Cromwell declared that he felt no personal animosity towards the majority of the Scots, whom he regarded as his Protestant brothers. He appealed to them to consider 'in the bowels of Christ' whether they were not grossly mistaken in opposing the English parliament. Even after setting out on his march north, Cromwell continued to issue conciliatory addresses to the Scots; he spoke of his 'longing to have avoided blood in this business'. It has been suggested that this explains the relative uncertainty of his military judgements during the Scottish campaign. In August he was frequently outmanoeuvred by David Leslie, the commander of the Covenanter forces. But whatever Cromwell's minor tactical errors may have been, when the two armies did finally meet at Dunbar, early in September, his military genius reasserted itself.

Cromwell's defeat of the Covenanter army at the battle of Dunbar is widely regarded by military historians as the greatest single achievement in his career as a soldier. Despite his army's being outnumbered by two to one and initially having been in a potentially disastrous position, his coolness under fire, perception, and power to inspire his troops, won a crushing victory. The Covenanters were left broken and dispirited; many of them interpreted their defeat as a sign of God's anger at their having dared to fight on Charles II's behalf.

Dunbar did not mark the end of the Scottish campaign. Cromwell remained in Scotland until well into 1651, but then, as he had in Ireland, he left subordinate generals to complete the subjugation. John Lambert and George Monk carried out the task ruthlessly and successfully.

Yet Charles II did not allow the crushing of the Covenanters to destroy his own hopes. In a bold, perhaps desperate, move, he tried to achieve in England what he failed to do in Scotland. With a force of 12,000 he marched south into England, trusting that his personal presence would inspire a royalist rising. It was not to be; the response was slight and ill-organised, and it was a despondent royalist army that finally confronted Cromwell's forces at Worcester on 3 September 1651, the anniversary of Dunbar. This time the strategic position was reversed. Cromwell had the overwhelming superiority in manpower and used it efficiently to rout the royalists. Charles accepted defeat and after eluding near capture fled abroad into an exile that was to last nine years.

The Rump proceeded to declare that Scotland was now totally subordinated to its authority. The Edinburgh parliament was dissolved and the power of the Presbyterian church was greatly reduced; it was ordered to tolerate the existence of the individual protestant sects in Scotland. In addition, the Scottish people were required to pay for the upkeep of the English army of occupation. It was the Rump's belief that these measures would extinguish for good the embers of royalism in Scotland.

6 The Record of the Rump

Until relatively recently, the Rump Parliament had had a very poor press. It tended to be regarded as an inefficient, self-perpetuating oligarchy, which clung to power for four years, until it was forcibly dissolved by an exasperated Oliver Cromwell in April 1653. However, modern researches, most prominently those of David Underdown, Blair Worden and Austin Woolrych, have led to an adjustment of this generally dismissive view of the Rump.

It is important to appreciate the magnitude of the difficulties that the Rump faced. The execution of Charles I meant that for the first time in English history a parliament became directly responsible for governing the nation. After 1649 the Rump Parliament combined both executive and legislative powers, functions which previously had always been separated. This created problems which ultimately proved too great for it to solve.

a) Religious Policy

The civil wars had left the position and character of the established church uncertain and confused. In 1645 Parliament had recommended the adoption of Presbyterianism, but had made no consistent effort to enforce this. The Rump Parliament was divided on the issue. The Presbyterians, with their desire for a centrally-controlled state church, were roughly equal in number to the Independents, who stood for the principle of permitting the local congregations (sometimes referred to as 'the gathered churches') to pursue their own form of worship. So evenly split was the Rump that it required the casting vote of the Speaker to defeat a proposal in August 1649 that Presbyterianism should be confirmed as the state religion of England. In addition to the two main groups there was a number of MPs who cannot be easily labelled, except by such confusing terms as 'independent Presbyterians', who favoured some form of compromise such as maintaining a central church while denying it a controlling authority over the local congregations. This was a notion with which Oliver Cromwell sympathised (see page 65).

What is clear is that, in keeping with the predominantly conservative mood, few members wished society to be left completely free in matters of morality. The majority of MPs were more concerned to take the opportunity provided by the establishment of the Commonwealth to impose 'godliness' (a code of moral conduct) upon the nation than to allow liberty of conscience. A series of acts was introduced imposing penalties on adultery, fornication and profane language. 'An Act against Blasphemy' was passed in 1650 with the aim of curbing the more extreme sectarians, such as the Ranters who claimed that since they belonged to the ranks of the godly they could do no wrong and therefore were not subject to the law (see page 61). The lack of more-sweeping measures indicated that the Rump had no real intention of reforming the church along the lines hoped for by the religious radicals. It was with some reluctance, and not until late in 1650, that the Rump finally repealed the statutes passed in Elizabeth's reign that had required Sunday worship in the Anglican church. On the vexed questions of tithes (taxes levied for the upkeep of the clergy), the Rump did nothing; the clergy continued to be paid in the old way.

Since the days of Laud it had been abundantly clear that control of the pulpit was the key factor in determining what form of worship was followed in the localities. The appointment of the clergy was, therefore, a vital concern and the Rump frequently discussed how this could best be organised. However, precisely because it was such a sensitive question, no clear decision was attainable. It is true that 'A Committee for the Propagation of the Gospel' was appointed by the Rump in 1652, with the intention of creating a system of strict supervision of clerical appointments. But the wide divisions within parliament over religion meant that no agreement could be reached over the standards to be applied in measuring the acceptability and reliability of individual clerics.

There is no doubt that in the country at large the dramatic events leading to the king's defeat and execution had encouraged the growth of millenarianism, the belief that the excitement of the times betokened a great cataclysm such as the the second coming of Christ on earth. Some believed that since the end of the world was imminent, the old forms of church and government should be jettisoned (see page 40). As a body the Rump did not represent this attitude. In the matter of religion, as in politics, its basic conservatism meant that it resisted the calls of the radicals for a complete break with the past. On the contrary, the Rump imposed a form of press censorship in an attempt to limit the flood of millenarian broadsheets and pamphlets that appeared in London and elsewhere. To counter criticism and to give an official version of what was going on, the Rump published its own government journal, *Mercurius Politicus.*

b) Legal and Social Policies

Demands for reform of the law were heard from sectarians, Levellers and the army. These interest groups were divided in what they wanted from reform, but they agreed that the existing legal system had to be changed. The main objections to the current legal practice was that it was the preserve of the privileged, prohibitively expensive, and scandalously slow in operation. The lawyers themselves were widely despised as corrupt manipulators. The law as it stood was seen by many radicals as an expression of the Norman yoke that had oppressed Englishmen and denied them their freedom since the days of William the Conqueror. Reformers called upon the Rump to curb the power of the lawyers and open the law to all by simplifying its arcane procedures. The Rump spent a considerable time discussing law reform; among its positive steps was the adoption of more lenient methods for punishing debtors and the authorisation of the use of English in the courts instead of Latin and French. But it did nothing to ensure lower legal fees or to provide easier access to the courts for the ordinary person.

An interesting aspect of the period is that the day-to-day operation of the law in the communities continued largely unchanged, a testimony to the underlying strength and stability of local institutions, and a reminder that the decisions of central government did not always determine what actually happened at local level.

The Rump's reluctance to consider major changes in the law is largely explained by the composition of the Commons. Of the 211 MPs who attended the House during the Commonwealth period, nearly 50 were from the legal profession. The largest single group among the average of 60-70 members who attended the daily sessions of parliament was composed of lawyers. Such men were naturally reluctant to undertake changes that would weaken their privileged position.

The same was true of the another interest group, which was strongly represented in the Commons, the merchants and traders. They used their influence to prevent interference with current commercial practices, such as monopolies, and were instrumental in the Rump's passing of the Navigation Act of 1651 (see page 76). What was true of the legal and commercial interests applied to the Rump overall. It contained few dedicated republicans intent on sweeping change. Its predominant aim was to gain the support of the established classes in society. A policy of moderation and regard for existing structures was far more likely to win over men of influence and authority in the localities. It was the provincial gentry, the traditional ruling order, whom the Rump were trying to impress.

The Rump did give some attention to proposals for social reform, which included schemes for the extension of education and for some form of poor relief. How genuine their interest was in this area cannot be easily assessed since in practice the demands of war and the maintenance of national security deprived them of both the time and the resources to turn such proposals into reality. Derek Hirst has said of the Rump that 'it always found the doing of business more urgent than the luxury of reform'.

c) Financial Policies

Judged by the amount of revenue it acquired, the Rump was a successful administrative body. It raised finance through taxation, assessment (taxes on land), excise levies, and the sale of Crown lands and church property. These were supplemented by the proceeds of confiscated royalist estates. This last policy, however, while being a useful source of revenue proved politically short-sighted since it made it difficult for royalists to reconcile themselves to the Commonwealth. Confiscation also contravened the spirit of the Pardon and Oblivion Act, which had been passed in 1652 with the intention of winning over those who had previously supported Charles I

Largely successful though its financial policies were, the Rump still remained short of money. Its revenue could not keep up with the cost of the campaigns in Ireland and Scotland and of the war against the Dutch (see page 76). It is important to stress how much of the Rump's time and revenue was spent on running the various wars in which it was engaged. The pressure of war is a factor that has to be borne in mind in any assessment of the Rump's record. The Rump cannot be said to have failed through want of trying. If anything, it tried too hard. As its legislative record shown below indicates, there are clear signs that its energies had begun to flag by 1653. For four years it had been in almost constant session, sitting four or five days a week throughout the year.

The Rump Parliament in action

Total number of Members who attended the House
between 1649 and 1653
211

Active members   Average attendance
60-70   50-60

Number of Legislative Committees Established
152 in 1649   98 in 1650   61 in 1651   51 in 1652   12 in 1653

Number of Acts passed
125 in 1649   78 in 1650   54 in 1651   44 in 1652   10 in 1653

% of legislation devoted to particular issues
security and finance - 51%   local government and the army - 30%
social problems - 9%   economic and social reform - 4%
religion - 3%   law reform - 3%

Since it was in the unprecedented position of being both a government and a parliament, the Rump had no clear administrative lines to guide it. Much of its work was done through committees, but there was no precise pattern of business, and co-ordination between the committees was uncertain. The boundaries of authority between the Council of State and the Commons were not sharply drawn, a situation which was partly explained by the fact that the Council was largely made up of sitting MPs.

It was not so much the administrative mistakes of the Commonwealth that weakened it, as the assumption by both the sectarians and the republicans that the Rump was merely a stage on the road to either the rule of the saints or of a full-blown republic. In view of the pressures on it from outside and its own internal divisions, and bearing in mind the extent of the administrative, financial and military burdens it carried, it was remarkable that the Rump was able to achieve four and and a half years of stable government. Nor must it be forgotten that the Rump's subjugation of Ireland and Scotland and the consolidation of its authority over them rank as extraordinary achievements by any measure.

7 The Dissolution of the Rump, April 1653

The Rump was never expected to be a permanent body. Indeed, in September 1651 it had made provision for its own dissolution, voting by a small majority to disband itself by the end of 1654. It had also set up a committee to supervise the drafting of plans for 'a new representative' parliament.

The Army Council was not impressed by this. It considered that the Rump had subsequently amended the qualifications for parliamentary elections in such a way as to ensure that the existing members would retain their seats. The notion that the Rump was manoeuvring to prevent a genuinely new parliament being elected offended the two main groups who had become increasingly disillusioned with the Commonwealth - the republicans, whose main spokesman was Colonel John Lambert, and the Fifth Monarchists, whose leader was Colonel Thomas Harrison. Both men had personal reasons for disliking the Rump since each felt he had been slighted by being denied promotions within the regime's gift.

However, in the event, it was Oliver Cromwell who forcibly ended the life of the Rump. Considerable research has been conducted into his motives. Not all historians who have studied the the question are in agreement. Nevertheless, the broad lines of the story can be established. What appears to have happened is that in April 1653 the Rump, rather than planning to perpetuate its existence, had actually begun to consider a bill that would have brought forward its dissolution by over a year. However, the army's fear was that this was simply a ruse to disguise the fact that the qualifications being written into the bill would result in any new parliament being composed of substantially the same members.

Whether the army's judgement was accurate cannot be known because the only copy of the bill was torn up by Cromwell at the time he dissolved the Rump. Cromwell's anger seems to have been aroused not so much by the bill itself but by the Rump's going back on a promise they had previously given him that they would suspend their consideration of it. On 20 April he marched to Westminster at the head of a column of troopers, entered the Commons, and told the startled members that their sitting was permanently at an end and that they must leave. "You have sat here too long for the good you do. In the name of God, go!". After a token protest by a few MPs, they did as they were told. The next day some wag nailed a notice to the door of the Commons a notice that read: "This House is to be let, now unfurnished".

Cromwell's role was obviously the critical one in the ending of the rule of the Rump, but it is important not to anticipate events by assuming that his eventual move had always been part of his plans. For the whole of the period 1649-53 he had remained the servant of parliament, a position which he loyally accepted, as shown by the letters and reports that throughout the Irish and Scottish campaigns he faithfully sent to the Speaker. Moreover, the evidence suggests that, notwithstanding the firmness with which he acted in April 1653, he had genuinely agonised over the decision to use force to end the Rump. While it is true that after Pride's Purge in 1648 the Rump was dependent for its existence on the goodwill of the army, it would be wrong to think of the army as a constant threat to parliament. Indeed, although it often urged MPs to pursue certain courses of action, the army rarely attempted to impose its will directly upon the Commons.

A striking example of this, was parliament's consistent refusal to accept the army's *Heads of Proposals,* first drawn up in 1647, as a basis for constitutional reform. The Proposals which included a programme of parliamentary, legal and financial reforms, as well as plans for the final settlement of the arrears owed to the army, was still being pressed upon the Rump as late as 1652. John Kenyon suggests that this 'astonishing demonstration of the army's impotence' is an important corrective to the notion of the Rump's existing for four years under the shadow of the military. One reason for the army's restraint was its pre-occupation for three years with the Scottish and Irish wars. Another is the attitude of its Commander-in-Chief. Right up to the time he dissolved parliament, Cromwell appears to have have wanted the Rump to succeed. Whatever radicalism may have attached to his religious ideas, his social and political views were conservative. As his later rule as Protector was to show, he never lost his belief in parliament as an essential part of any constitutional settlement. He held his army in check until his disgust with the Rump at their betrayal of his hopes overcame him.

Pride's Purge - the trial and execution of the king

Commonwealth 1649-53

Rump Parliament > | < Council of the Army

threats to the Commonwealth
Levellers   religious radicals

the Commonwealth consolidated
Cromwell subdues Ireland   Scotland subordinated

the Record of the Rump

policies	achievements	weaknesses
social and economic religious foreign	4 years of government control of 3 kingdoms	impermanence dependence on army financial strains

forcibly dissolved by Cromwell, 1653

Summary - The Rump Parliament, 1649-53

Making notes on *'The Rump Parliament, 1649-53'*

Even a cursory reading of this chapter will indicate that a great deal happened in the years, 1649-53. It is important not to get lost in detail; the sub-sections into which the chapter is divided offer a convenient way of concentrating on essential developments. There are four essential aspects of the story to grasp.

1 the establishment of the Commonwealth and the rule of the Rump from 1649 to 1653. Sections 1, 2 and 3 are the relevant ones in this respect. A helpful way of setting out your notes is:

Heading - the Rule of the Rump

Sub-Headings

the Rump's view of itself / The Army's Attitude / the Rump's enemies

Under each of these sub-headings you should then jot down the principal points, as given in the sub-sections. Under the first column, for example, might go: Rump regarded itself as the supreme constitutional authority - claimed to represent the nation - saw the army as its protector, not its master. Under the third column it would be appropriate to list: from the beginning - religious and political radicals, republicans; later - exasperated army officers, e.g., Cromwell.

2 Why the Rump was able to overcome the Leveller threat. This involves your understanding the reasons for the decline of the Levellers in 1649; the reasons will include the weakness of the movement itself and the determination of Cromwell to break it by force. Section 3 is the relevant one. Again, the heading/sub-columns pattern of notes is recommended

3 The Cromwellian subjugation of Ireland and Scotland: sections 4 and 5 will give you the main reasons why neither country was able to resist the Rump's army under Cromwell. This involves your understanding the relative weakness of the Irish and Scots as well as Cromwell's strength. Three appropriate columns for notes would be: Irish weaknesses, Scottish weaknesses, Cromwell's strength.

4 The record of the Rump - with particular reference to the material in Sections 6 and 7. A number of sub-columns for your notes is called for here. Some possibilities are:

The Rump's Record

Policies	Internal Weakness	Outside Pressures	Relations with Army

---

Source-based questions on 'The Rump Parliament, 1649-53'

1 Cromwell and the Levellers
Read the extracts from John Lilburne's statement on pages 18-19. Answer the following questions:
a) Examine the meaning of the following terms, as used by Cromwell: 'the guilt and blood and treasure shed and spent in this kingdom' (lines 2-3). (2 marks)
    'a despicable, contemptible generation of men' (lines 8-9). (3 marks)
b) Using your own knowledge, examine the ways in which Cromwell fulfilled his own admonition that 'you have no other way to deal with these men but to break them' (lines 1-2). (7 marks)
c) Assess the strength and weaknesses of this source as evidence of Cromwell's attitude towards the Levellers. (8 marks)

2 Cromwell in Ireland
Study the extracts from Cromwell's reports on pages 25-6, and from his Declaration on pages 26-7. Answer the following questions:
a) Explain the meaning of the following in the context in which they appear:

'it will tend to prevent the effusion of blood for the future' (lines 14-15, page 26). (3 marks)
'the Undeceiving of deluded and seduced People' (line 2, page 26). (3 marks)
'You are part of Antichrist' (line 3, page 26)(3 marks)
b) In his reports, on pages 25-6, how does Cromwell justify his post-siege treatment of the inhabitants of Drogheda and Wexford? (6 marks)
c) Using your own knowledge and the evidence in the sources, examine the reasons why Cromwell was so ferocious in his attitude towards the Catholic Irish. (7 marks)
d) In what ways are these sources valuable to the historian as evidence of the strength and nature of religious beliefs in this period? (8 marks)

CHAPTER 3

The Search for a Settlement, 1653-8

1 The Nominated Assembly, July-December 1653

The dissolution of the Rump had also been accompanied by the dispersal of the Council of State. This meant that England was indisputably under direct military rule. Yet, although Cromwell and the Army Council now held power, they immediately took steps to try to restore constitutional forms. On behalf of the Army Council, Cromwell announced that a new assembly was to be established, not by election but by nomination. After his officers had vetted lists of reliable persons in the localities, he issued the following summons to 140 selected individuals:

1 Forasmuch as, upon the dissolution of the late Parliament, it became necessary that the peace, safety, and good government of this Commonwealth should be provided for; and in order thereunto, divers persons fearing God and of approved integrity
5 and honesty are, by myself, with the advice of my Council of Officers, nominated; to whom the great charge and trust of so weighty affairs is to be committed; and having good assurance of your love to, and courage for, God and the interest of his cause and of the good people of the Commonwealth; I, Oliver Cromwell,
10 Captain General and Commander-in-Chief of all the armies and forces raised and to be raised within this Commonwealth, do hereby summon you to be and appear at the Council Chamber at Whitehall upon the fourth day of July next ... then and there to take upon you the said trust; unto which you are hereby called and
15 appointed.

The reference to 'persons fearing God' led to the assembly's being described to as the 'Parliament of the Saints'. Alternative names by which it became known include: the 'Nominated Assembly', the 'Little Parliament' and 'Barebone's Parliament'. This last title came from the attempt by royalists and republicans to ridicule the assembly, whose legitimacy they refused to accept, by naming it after one of its back bench members, Praise-God Barebone, a London leather-seller.

As the wording of the summons shows, the Nominated Assembly represented Cromwell's attempt to achieve stable rule in England by entrusting government to the godly. This used to be interpreted by historians as a concession to the ideas of Harrison and the Fifth Monarchists, who had urged that a body structured like the sanhedrin (council) of the ancient Israelites should be instituted. However, modern writers have seen it more as a compromise between the ideas of Harrison and those of John Lambert, the leading republican, who had wanted government to be carried on, in the interim before a full republic could be established, by a council nominated by the army. In its final form, the 140-member Assembly was exactly twice the size of the sanhedrin model, which enabled it to appear more representative than a smaller body would have been.

As with the Rump earlier, the new assembly was not intended to be permanent. This is clear from its decision to fix a date, November 1654, for its own dissolution. At the time of its first gathering in July, the assembly appointed a new Council of State of 31 members; this contained a number of officers, including Cromwell, but the majority was made up of civilians. Soon after it first met the Assembly voted to declare itself a parliament. This was not what Cromwell had intended and was the first sign that the Assembly was not going to satisfy his expectations.

The fact that the army had selected the members of the assembly did not result in a quiescent house. From the beginning there was a sizable minority of members who refused to be overawed by the military. These were largely Fifth Monarchists and sectarian fanatics who seriously believed that their task was to prepare the way for Christ's coming. This led them in their wildest moments to demand the sweeping away of all forms of organised religion and the abolition of all existing law. This implied a rejection of the social order and the rights of property. Although the fanatics were a minority, their extremism overshadowed proceedings and tended to be taken as characteristic of the Assembly as a whole during its five-months existence. The moderates and conservative members eventually grew exasperated with the extremists and concluded that the only way to check their fervour was to dissolve the Assembly. Accordingly, in December, the moderates outmanoeuvred the radicals by meeting in a special session, from which the latter were excluded, and voting to terminate their proceedings. In this way they returned to Cromwell the authority he had granted them.

The tame ending of the Nominated Assembly should not be taken to mean that it had been a total failure. It is true that it disappointed the hopes of reformers. Cromwell later referred to his calling of the Nominated Assembly as 'a story of my own weakness and folly' and admitted that 'these 140 honest men could not govern'. But scholars now recognise that the Assembly had progressive aspects. Gerald Aylmer regards the work of the Assembly as a seminal period in the development of public administration in England. Among the proposals which it discussed in the 15 committees into which it divided were the reform of the law on debt, humane treatment of the insane, the civil registration of births deaths and marriages, and greater protection for travellers on the highways. In many respects these measures were ahead of their time. After the Restoration it became customary to dismiss this

Assembly as if it had been composed simply of incompetent and inexperienced social upstarts. This was a false picture. Austin Woolrych has made a detailed study of the Nominated Assembly's composition; among his important findings are the following:

- 116 of the members ranked as gentry (substantial landowners),
- 119 members were JPs in their local communities,
- 40 members had attended university, while another 40 had trained as lawyers,
- 24 members had sat in a previous parliament, and 67 would be elected to later parliaments,
- nearly all the members had some form of administrative experience.

There are good grounds, therefore, for speculating that had the Nominated Assembly not been riven by the religious issue it would have performed as effectively as any of the other parliaments of the period. Like them its stability was fatally weakened by its failure to reconcile social conservatism and religious fanaticism.

2 The Founding of the Protectorate

a) The *Instrument of Government*, December 1653

Cromwell later claimed to have known 'not one tittle' about the manoeuvre by which the moderates had outwitted the religious fanatics and ended the life of the Nominated Assembly. This is doubtful; the signs are that he had already lost faith in it. He had been displeased in particular by its proposal to end the monthly assessment (property tax), a move which he interpreted as an attack upon the army, since it was the assessment on which the upkeep of the army depended. What is certain is that he was fully aware of the *Instrument of Government,* the alternative constitution that had been drawn up even before the Assembly dissolved itself. This was the work of John Lambert, one of the brightest of the younger officers, who for some time had been pressing for a written constitution that would give solidity and stability to the republic.

The *Instrument* provided for a Lord Protector, who was to hold executive powers and be aided by a Council of State, and a single-chamber parliament of 400 members from England and Wales that was to meet at least once every three years for a minimum of three months. In addition, Ireland and Scotland were to be represented in the House by 30 MPs apiece, thus making it the first-ever truly British parliament. In a direct repudiation of Leveller ideas, the *Instrument* stipulated that the franchise was to be restricted to men of substance. The possession of property or income of a value of at least £200 was made the basic qualification for voting. Papists and known royalists were declared ineligible to vote or to seek election. In an attempt to settle the religious question, the *Instrument* declared somewhat imprecisely that there was to be a national church professing 'sound doctrine'. Liberty of worship was to be the right of 'such as profess faith in God by Jesus Christ', with the exception of papists and those guilty of 'licentiousness', a reference to extreme sectarians. The *Instrument* also declared that there was to be a standing (permanent) army of 30,000 soldiers.

b) Cromwell's Position as Lord Protector

The speed and smoothness with which the *Instrument* was adopted indicates that Cromwell was well prepared for it. In November he had held discussions with Lambert and the army officers, and had keenly supported the drafting of a new constitution, provided it did not involve his being made 'King Oliver'. Cromwell's objection was meant to scotch rumours that had been circulating for some months that he contemplated being made emperor or king. Cromwell preferred the renewal of the title of 'Lord Protector' since this office had a number of precedents in English history going back to the fifteenth century. This is a clear example of his wish to maintain links with the ancient constitution, while at the same distancing himself from the recently disgraced and overthrown monarchy.

Within four days of the ending of the Nominated Assembly, the *Instrument* had begun to operate and Cromwell had been installed as Lord Protector. During the following nine months, before the meeting of the first parliament of the Protectorate in September 1654, Cromwell worked with the Council of State in drafting a large number of ordinances which he intended to present to parliament for ratification. The measures covered a wide range. They included financial reform and the regularising of the two main types of taxation in operation, the 'assessment', which was a monthly locally-raised tax on property, and the 'excise', a centrally-imposed tax on goods and commodities.

Other ordinances of importance were those concerned with religious reorganisation (see page 65) and those carrying forward the legal and administrative reforms, first suggested but not implemented under the Rump. Cromwell regarded sound laws as essential to the well-being of the nation and recognised that it was their unjust application that caused their unpopularity.

> 1 There is one general Grievance in the Nation. It is the Law ... and
> the great grievance lies in the execution and administration ... To
> hang a man for six pence, thirteen pence, I know not what; to hang
> for a trifle, and pardon murder - is the ministration of the Law,
> 5 through the ill-framing of it.

While there was no doubting that the Protectorate had now become the effective constitution, its legality remained in question throughout its six-year existence (1653-9). The *Instrument of Government* from which the Protectorate derived its authority was solely the product of the Council of Officers; it was never given full civilian backing and was never formally ratified by any of the parliaments called during these years. It was a governmental system imposed by the military, and it is evident that Cromwell remained conscious of this throughout his time as Lord Protector. This is worth stressing, for it acts as a corrective to the notion that the Protectorate parliaments were merely obstructive bodies standing in the way of reform and progress. The MPs who challenged the *Instrument* and Cromwell's authority under it had as much or as little right to do so as the Army Council had in imposing it. After all, parliament could claim that it was an elected body, whereas the Army Council represented nobody but themselves.

3 The First Protectorate Parliament, September 1654-January 1655

Under the terms of the *Instrument* a parliament was scheduled to meet in September 1654. The elections for it took place during the preceding summer months. There is no clear evidence that the army made a determined effort to interfere with the elections, which Gerald Aylmer judges to have been 'as free as any in the seventeenth century'. Certainly the results did not return a House submissive to Cromwell and the army. The 460 members included Presbyterians, republicans, and even some royalist sympathisers. The decision taken in accordance with the *Instrument* to transfer seats to the more populous counties at the expense of the corrupt borough constituencies had the important effect of increasing the number of independent county-gentry members.

Cromwell had hoped that the new parliament would quickly accept and implement the ordinances that he and the Council of State had drafted. He was to be disappointed. Although in his opening address he reminded the assembled MPs that their first duty was to provide the people of England with 'good and wholesome laws', the new parliament gave priority not to considering reform but to attacking the *Instrument*. The republican MPs (Commonwealthsmen), those who claimed that Cromwell's dissolution of the Rump had been unlawful, led the attack. They challenged the right of the Protector to exercise the degree of civil and military authority granted him by the *Instrument*, and criticised the composition of the Council of State, complaining particularly that it contained too many army officers. They also expressed their dislike of the military by objecting to the high cost of maintaining the standing army that had been sanctioned by the *Instrument*. They demanded that it be reduced from 50,000 to 30,000, as stipulated in the new constitution.

It had been Cromwell's declared wish that this parliament would begin 'healing and settling' the religious differences that divided the nation. However, far from taking a conciliatory line, parliament voiced its concern at the amount of toleration that had already been allowed under the Protectorate. Cromwell tried to lessen the growing opposition by obliging the MPs to take an oath of loyalty to the Protectorate. This resulted in the exclusion of 100 members who refused to swear allegiance, but it did not greatly diminish the criticism of his regime. None of the 84 ordinances which Cromwell had previously prepared was passed by parliament. Nor was it content simply to obstruct his proposals. It openly sought to restrict his powers as Protector by introducing a new constitutional bill which would have effectively undermined the authority granted him under the *Instrument*. This proved the final straw for Cromwell; in January 1654 he dissolved parliament after just five months sitting. When doing so he defined four 'fundamentals' on which he believed government should rest:

1 Government by a Single Person and a Parliament is a fundamental!
  That Parliaments should not make themselves perpetual is a fundamental
  Is not liberty of conscience a fundamental?
5 The army should not have absolute power; neither should that authority which governs the army have absolute power - that is a fundamental

4 The Major-Generals, 1655-7

1655 was a critical year for the Protectorate. In addition to the failure of parliament to fulfil Cromwell's hopes, royalist and republican opposition threatened in the country at large (see page 67). Rumours of Leveller or republican plots to assassinate the Lord Protector circulated widely. These dangers encouraged Cromwell to look to his natural allies, the army commanders, as a way of ensuring not simply military security, but administrative efficiency as well. This led to the introduction of a system of direct military government, known as the rule of the Major-Generals. The decision to adopt this experiment was not Cromwell's alone, but was taken after lengthy consultation with the Army Council. John Lambert, who was himself to be one of the Major-Generals, was a leading proponent of the scheme. In the late summer of 1655, England was divided into 11 (subsequently 12) districts, each one under the jurisdiction of a Major-General, responsible not only for exercising military control but also for overseeing the operation of local government.

The Major-Generals and their Jurisdiction
John Barkstead - Middlesex
James Berry - Wales and Worcestershire

William Butler - Northants, Huntingdonshire, Bedfordshire
John Desborough - Gloucs, Wiltshire, Dorset, Somerset,
Devon, Cornwall
Charles Fleetwood - Norfolk, Suffolk, Essex
William Gough - Berkshire, Hampshire, Sussex
Thomas Kelsey - Surrey and Kent
John Lambert - Yorks, Cumberland, Westmoreland,
Northumberland
William Packer - Oxfordshire, Buckinghamshire
Philip Skippon - London
Edward Whalley - Derby, Notts, Lincoln, Warwickshire,
Leicestershire
Charles Worsley - Lancashire, Cheshire and Staffordshire

In their official Instructions the Major-Generals were granted
unprecedentedly wide powers and duties:

1 1 They are to endeavour the suppressing [of] all tumults,
insurrections, rebellions or other unlawful assemblies which shall be
within the said counties respectively ...
2 They are to take care and give order, that all papists and others who
5 have been in arms against the parliament, or assisted the late king or
his son in the late wars, as also all others who are dangerous to the
peace of the nation, be disposed of, as may be for the public service ...
6 They shall in their constant carriage and conversation encourage
and promote godliness and virtue, and discourage and discoun-
10 tenance all profaneness and ungodliness; and shall endeavour with
the other justices of the peace, and other ministers and officers who
are entrusted with the care of those things, that the laws against
drunkenness, blaspheming and taking of the name of God in vain, by
swearing and cursing, plays and interludes, and profaning the Lord's
15 Day, and such-like wickedness and abominations, be put in more
effectual execution than they have been hitherto ...
19 ... that all gaming houses and houses of evil fame [brothels] be
industriously sought out and suppressed within the cities of London
and Westminster and all the liberties thereof ...
20 21 That all alehouses, taverns and victualling houses towards the
outskirts of the said cities ... be suppressed, except such as are
necessary and convenient to travellers; and that the number of
alehouses in all other parts of the town be abated, and none continued
but such as can lodge strangers and are of good repute.

The most striking part of the work of the Major-Generals was the
introduction of the Decimation Tax, a 10 per cent levy imposed on
known royalists who had annual incomes of more than £100. The

measure was intended both to prevent further risings, such as Penruddock's which occurred in March 1655 (see page 67), and to raise revenue for the upkeep of the rule of the Major-Generals, who had authority to raise local troops in order to maintain the army's strength. The hope was that in this way the new tax would be the means both of preserving a powerful standing army and avoiding a heavy charge on central government funds.

Although for the sake of convenience historians have tended to generalise about the rule of the Major-Generals as if it were a single system, the type of administration in each of the 12 districts was determined very much by the degree of zeal with which the individual Major-General chose to carry out his instructions. For example, Whalley, Kelsey and Worsley (who is reputed to have closed down over 200 ale-houses), were renowned for their industry and sense of duty while Gough openly acknowledged that he was not up to the task.

What appears to have made the Major-Generals particularly unpopular was their interference with ordinary life in the localities, especially their attempt, in accordance with Instruction 6, to impose moral behaviour upon the inhabitants. Moreover, their military rank could not disguise the fact that they were of a lower social status than the local gentry over whom they had been placed. For local magistrates and officials who functioned in what was very much a hierarchical order, the intrusion of social upstarts into the conduct of affairs was particularly distasteful.

In addition, few of the Major-Generals were local to the area over which they exercised authority. This created a strong feeling among the people in the communities that they were now subject to outside rule. One of the features of mid-seventeenth century England on which modern historians are agreed is that local loyalties predominated over national ones. National consciousness did exist, as the popular support for foreign wars often indicated, but people's first thoughts were for their own local concerns. Consequently when directly- intrusive government was imposed from outside, no matter how well-intentioned or efficient, it ran counter to the taste and tradition of the localities. It was this that stood in the way of the total acceptance of the Major-Generals and the Protectorate that had appointed them.

The difficulties that this created for Cromwell illustrate the limited control that he actually exercised as Protector. His authority was considerable but it was never absolute. Barry Coward, has observed:

1 The contribution of Cromwell and the Council [of State] to the stability and efficiency of the government of England in the 1650s is, of course, limited. Their personal intervention in favour of 'healing and settling' and reform were spasmodic and did not
5 amount to a co-ordinated 'policy' of centralisation; nor did they have the bureaucratic machinery to carry one out.

The same limitation applied to the Major-Generals. The apparent strictness of their rule and the resentment it aroused have been customarily taken as evidence of their effectiveness as centralising administrators. Derek Hirst, an authority on the period, has doubted this interpretation. He has written that, 'the assumption that the major-generals represent the high point of early-modern centralisation is open to question ... historians have been misled by the intensity of the major-generals' labours'.

The evidence suggests that during the 1650s local institutions continued to function effectively regardless of the political changes and developments that took place at the centre. Magistrates courts operated as they had done before the Civil Wars. In the previous decade county committees appointed by parliament had largely replaced the traditional rule of local Justices of the Peace. However, the decision of the Rump to cease funding the county committees had seen their disappearance and the re-emergence of the JPs as the principal local administrative system. In any case, Cromwell had no wish to undermine the authority of the leaders in the communities; it would have suited him far better if the Major-Generals could have established harmonious relations with the local gentry. However, if that was the intention, it failed since the system had begun to founder on the rock of local resistance long before Cromwell had lost faith in it.

Given that Cromwell had at his disposal a large, professional, highly-successful and godly army, there was a logic to his attempt to use it to take a further step towards the creation of a godly nation. He claimed in a speech to parliament in September 1656 that the system of Major-Generals had been 'very effectual towards the discountenancing of vice and settling religion, than anything else these fifty years'. This was wishful thinking. Religion had not been settled. Furthermore, the unpopularity that the regime had aroused outweighed whatever individual successes might have been achieved. Although it had not been Cromwell's intention, the rule of the Major-Generals had challenged the independence of the local gentry; it had imposed taxes and raised local militia without parliamentary authority and with little reference to the opinion of the leaders in the community. In the parliamentary elections, held in the summer of 1656, the protest slogan 'no swordsmen, no decimators' was often and widely voiced, an indication of how unpopular the Major-Generals had become.

The Major-Generals as a system of control were not part of the *Instrument of Government*. They were intended to fill the gap before the next parliament. They did not, therefore, take Cromwell any nearer to solving the problem of providing stable, non-military rule. Indeed, it seemed even clearer that stability and order depended on military authority. Christopher Hill uses a striking metaphor to describe this situation. He suggests that in spite of all Cromwell's efforts to legitimise his authority he was in the final analysis, 'sitting on bayonets and nothing else'.

5 The Second Protectorate Parliament, 1656-8

a) The First Session, September 1656-July 1657

The decision to summon a new parliament, a year earlier than was required under the *Instrument,* was prompted by the need to raise money. As with the Stuarts before him, Cromwell found it difficult to run the government on the income he was granted by his various parliaments. It was not that he was unduly extravagant. Although his wife and daughters liked to live in some style, Cromwell's Protectorate 'court' at Whitehall was certainly not lavish by royal standards. He himself lived relatively frugally.

Nonetheless, the administrative and military costs of maintaining the Protectorate were high. A parliamentary report in 1655 revealed that the government's annual revenue, made up from such sources as customs and excise, assessments and fines on royalists, amounted to £2,250,000, whereas military, naval and civil expenditure was £2,611,532. The deficit was increased by the added military costs occasioned by the war against Spain that began in 1656 (see page 78). It was the necessity of

Cromwell's wife, Elizabeth

raising extra finance that led the Major-Generals to advise Cromwell to call another parliament. They told him that they would be able to monitor the elections so as to ensure that only co-operative members would be returned.

Greater efforts were certainly made to shape the composition of the House than at the time of the first Protectorate parliament. When the new parliament met in September 1656, 100 members were declared ineligible and prevented from taking their seats. The early signs were that this purge had produced the desired result, the first months of the session proving relatively quiet. Indeed, Cromwell congratulated the members on their willingness to consider voting supplies (money) for the Spanish war and their ready attention to business. However, it was not long before friction occurred.

The first major difficulty arose over the House's prosecution for blasphemy of the Quaker, James Nayler. This was a matter in which parliament, in Cromwell's judgement, had exceeded its powers (see page 63). It was against this background of strained relations between Protector and parliament that the second crisis of the session occurred. In January 1657 John Desborough, the main spokesman for the Major-Generals, introduced a bill to renew the decimation tax for the maintenance of the militia in the counties. Since the upkeep of the Major-Generals depended upon this tax, to vote against the bill was to vote against the continuation of their regime. This is precisely what parliament proceeded to do. The defeat of Desborough's militia bill marked the effective end of the Major-Generals as a system of government. Cromwell's reaction was angry but, significantly, his anger was directed as much against the generals for having advised him to call parliament in the first place as against the MPs who had opposed the bill. He did not formally abandon the system of Major-Generals; it was simply allowed to lapse.

The reason why Cromwell did nothing to save the system deserves explanation for it helps to illustrate the ambiguous position in which he now found himself. Support for Cromwell at this point in his Protectorship came from two main sources. One obvious group was the army leaders, such as the Major-Generals, who saw him as a representative of themselves, someone concerned to use military strength as the guarantee of national security and effective government. Their experience ever since the civil wars had made them suspicious of all parliaments, which they regarded as self-seeking oligarchies rather than as guardians of liberty and the constitution.

The second group is identified by modern historians, most notably by Austin Woolrych, as 'new Cromwellians'. The term refers to those in public life who wished to see the Protectorate become an essentially civilian government. The group did include some important military figures: outstanding examples were General Monk, Cromwell's commander in Scotland, and Lord Broghill, a one-time royalist but now a staunch friend and confidant of Cromwell. However, it was made up largely of civilian politicians; leading lawyers such as Bulstrode Whitelocke and William Lenthall figured prominently among them. These men were traditionalists in that they believed in the virtues of the old constitution and the social order, but they were sufficiently flexible to accept that the Protectorate could be reshaped in such a way as to incorporate the social and political values that they prized. They held that the more Cromwell was able to distance himself from the military the closer he would move towards making the Protectorate an acceptable and permanent system of government. It would seem, therefore, that in allowing the rule of the Major Generals to fall into disuse Cromwell was responding to the wishes of the new Cromwellians.

b) The *Humble Petition and Advice,* 1657

The new Cromwellians formalised their views in a document which eventually became known as the *Humble Petition and Advice.* This was an alternative written constitution to the *Instrument of Government* and was offered to Cromwell in March 1657. It proposed that Cromwell should become king, be granted adequate financial resources, and rule with a restored Privy Council and with regular parliaments that would include an upper house. This renewal of kingship was meant not to extend Cromwell's authority but to limit it. What was envisaged was not the absolute monarchy which the Stuarts had tried to exercise before 1640, but a constitutional monarchy in which parliament would be an equal and permanent partner.

One aspect of the *Humble Petition and Advice* had an obvious attraction for Cromwell. Since the offer of the new constitution had come from parliament it would have a validity and legality that the *Instrument,* the creation of the Army Council, had lacked. He certainly gave the offer much thought. This is evident from a number of contemporary accounts. As early as 1652, Cromwell, in a conversation recorded by Bulstrode Whitelocke, had been mindful of the attractions of monarchy:

1 And surely the power of a king is so great and high and so universally understood and reverenced by the people of this nation that the title of it might not only indemnify in a great measure those that act under it, but likewise be of great use and advantage in such
5 times as these, to curb the insolences and extravagances of those whom the present powers cannot control.

During the spring of 1657 rumours that Cromwell was seriously considering accepting the offer of kingship led to a series of petitions from the army officers urging him to reject such a course. They appealed to him to remain faithful to 'the good old cause'.

One typical petition from the officers declared:

1 That they had hazarded their lives against the monarchy, and were still ready so to do in defence of the liberties of the nation; that having observed in some men great endeavours to bring the nation under the old servitude by pressing their General to take upon him
5 the title and government of a king, in order to destroy him and weaken the hands of those who were faithful to the public, they therefore humbly desired that [he] would discountenance all such persons and endeavours, and continue steadfast to the good old cause, for the preservation of which they for their parts were most
10 ready to lay down their lives.

After weeks of discussion and soul-searching, which he described as causing him great 'consternation of spirit', Cromwell finally informed parliament in April that he had decided not to accept the title of king. He offered the following reason:

1 It was said that kingship is not a title, but an office, so interwoven with the fundamental laws of the nation that they cannot, or cannot well, be executed and exercised without it - I cannot take upon me to repel these grounds; for they are strong and rational.
5 But if I shall be able to make any answer to them, I must not grant that they are necessarily conclusive: ... Truly the providences of God hath laid aside this title of king providentially and this not by sudden humour or passion; but it hath been by issue of as great deliberation as ever was in a nation. It hath been the issue of ten or
10 twelve years civil war wherein much blood hath been shed ... I will not seek to set up that that Providence hath destroyed and laid in the dust:

In the end, therefore, Cromwell had opted for what the army leaders called 'the good old cause'. Despite this, some sections of the army still remained uneasy about his intentions. Part of the problem was the long delay between the offer of the crown and his refusal of it. In Maurice Ashley's words, Cromwell's decision 'alienated his new friends while his prolonged hesitations displeased his old ones'.

Cromwell's rejection of the office of king was not a rejection of the proposed new constitution itself. In May he duly accepted the *Humble Petition* in a modified form. He was to remain 'His Highness, the Lord Protector Oliver' and was empowered to name his successor and to appoint the members of the 'Other' (upper) House. For some this was kingship in all but name. Edmund Ludlow, an ardent republican and representative of those Commonwealthsmen who had been suspicious of Cromwell's aims ever since his dissolution of the Rump in 1653, regarded the revised version of the *Humble Petition* as merely the climax of a Cromwellian plot to gain the Protector an unwarrantable extension of authority.

This now seems a harsh verdict. Cromwell's acceptance of the new constitution suggests how anxious he still was to reach a balanced settlement that would unite the whole nation. A number of his modern biographers have noted how often the word 'settlement' figured in his letters and speeches around this time. For example, addressing a parliamentary committee in April 1657, he said,

> 1 You have need to look at settlement. I would rather I were in my grave than hinder you on anything that may be for settlement, for the nation needs it and never needed it more ... I am hugely taken with the word Settlement, with the thing and with the notion of it. I
> 5 think he is not worthy to live in England that is not ... A nation is like a house, it cannot stand without settlement.

Cromwell's position as Protector under the new constitution adopted in 1657 represented a compromise. He had strengthened the civilian base of the Protectorate, but the army still remained the major force within it. This was clear in the way Cromwell used his authority as Protector to appoint a large number of his officer colleagues to seats in the Other House. Since this upper chamber of 40 members had the right to veto

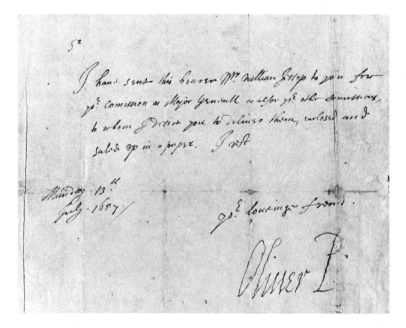

Cromwell's letter dismissing John Lambert

legislation of which it disapproved, it possessed considerable constitutional power. Republicans were swift to condemn an arrangement which subordinated the will of parliament to the whim of the army. They complained that the *Humble Petition and Advice* was no more than a tinkering with the existing system. It left Cromwell and the army in control.

At the end of July 1657, a month after Cromwell's second formal installation as Protector, parliament went into recess. Already there were signs that the adoption of the *Humble Petition* had not solved Cromwell's problems. He was obliged to dismiss from the Privy Council John Lambert, his long-standing colleague and the creator of the *Instrument of Government,* for refusing to take the oath of loyalty to the new constitution. It may well be Lambert acted out of career motives, hoping that by detaching himself from involvement in the new constitutional arrangements he would be in a strong position should they prove ineffective. But whatever Lambert's personal motives, the incident indicated that Cromwell had not succeeded in his aim of establishing a government representative of, and therefore acceptable to, a wide political spectrum.

c) The Second Session of Parliament, January-February 1658

The House of Commons that reassembled in January 1658 was significantly different from the one that had gone into recess six months earlier. The members who had been excluded at the beginning of the first session in September 1656 had returned. These were largely republicans. They had been debarred originally on the grounds that they were 'unfit' persons as defined by the *Instrument of Government.* But now that a new constitution had been adopted that technicality could no longer be invoked by the government to keep them out. Their return was an important victory for the republicans. Led by Arthur Haselrig, who believed that all government had been illegitimate since the dissolution of the Rump, they launched into an attack on the new constitution. Among their targets were the authority of the Protector, the power of the army, high taxation, and foreign policy.

Cromwell's difficulties were increased by the depletion of his supporters in the lower House, the most able of whom he had transferred to the Other House. Fearing that the parliamentary onslaught might lead to his political and religious enemies combining, he decided to end the sitting. His particular reason for dissolving parliament after a session of less than a month was to prevent its considering a republican petition that called for the abandonment of the Protectorate and the restoration of the Rump. Cromwell's deepest worry was that the petition was rumoured to have found favour with some of the troops.

6 Cromwell's Last Months

At the time of the dissolution of what proved to be his last parliament Cromwell had scarcely seven months to live. In traditional descriptions he is often portrayed in this period as an ageing man, weakened by illness, and in despair at his failure to achieve a settlement. The picture is exaggerated. While it is true that on occasion he was incapacitated by the malaria which he had contracted during his Irish campaigns, he remained highly active until at least the last month of his life. He supervised the workings of day-to-day government and paid particular attention to foreign policy. He had certainly not given up all hope of a settlement. His frequent discussions with the army officers and his readiness where necessary to dismiss those of doubtful loyalty showed his determination to preserve army unity and with it the nation's security. His greatest problems remained financial. The annual income of £1,300,000 that he had been granted under the *Humble Petition* was not enough to meet his governmental needs, which exceeded that sum by £500,000. As had Charles I before him, he found it increasingly difficult to raise loans from the City. This was no doubt why he drew up plans for the calling of parliament later in the year.

When Cromwell became Protector in 1653 he had faced a number of demanding questions. How was a stable executive government to be created to replace traditional monarchy? What was to be the place of parliament? Was the army to continue to play a political role? How was government to be effectively financed? How were the religious differences in the nation to be settled? At his death on 3 September 1658, these issues remained largely unresolved. Some sceptics have suggested that it was never his intention to resolve them; his essential aim, they argue, was to exercise power, not to reach settlements. Many contemporaries held that view and it has been restated periodically ever since. However, most modern historians lean to the view that to regard Cromwell simply as a military leader exercising authority for its own sake is to disregard the strength of his religious and political motivation. Even though he did not achieve his aim there is no sound reason to doubt the sincerity of his desire to reach a just and godly settlement.

Making Notes on 'The Search for a Settlement, 1653-8'

One way of understanding the developments covered in this chapter is to see them as a series of experiments aimed at achieving governmental stability. Take each of these experiments in turn (Nominated Assembly 1653, First Protectorate Parliament 1654-5, Major Generals 1655-7, Second Protectorate Parliament 1657-8) and break them down into manageable and memorable sections by posing three questions against each of them - a) What were the aims behind it? b) What were its main

Nominated Assembly 1653
creation of Cromwell and the army
taken over by religious radicals
moderates combine to dissolve it

Instrument of Government, 1653-7
Protectorate inaugurated
Lord Protector Cromwell and Council of State
Cromwell's Ordinances

First Protectorate Parliament, 1654-5
Cromwell's hopes of 'healing and settling' frustrated
Ordinances not implemented

Major-Generals, 1655-7
imposition of direct military rule
unwelcome in the localities
reaction against 'swordsmen and decimators'

Second Protectorate Parliament, 1656-8
criticise Cromwell and Major Generals
the Nayler case

Humble Petition and Advice, 1657-8
Cromwell declines kingship
Republicans and sectaries attack new constitution
Cromwell dies with constitutional issue unsettled

Summary - The Search for a Settlement, 1653-8

features? c) How far did it achieve its aims?

Cromwell of course looms large in all this; to gain an appreciation of his position and attitude pay close attention to the two written constitutions which he accepted and which defined his authority as Lord Protector. These were the *Instrument of Government* and the *Humble Petition and Advice*. List the main points in these in regard to the powers they granted to Cromwell and the restrictions they placed upon him. An example of an effective way of setting out your notes is:

Heading: Question
What were the aims behind the convening of the Nominated Assembly?
Answer: Main Aims - to provide:
godly rule | balanced government | a lower army profile

The same type of question and answer formula can be used in relation to each of the other sections.

Source-based questions on 'The Search for a Settlement, 1653-8'

1 The Cromwellian Principles of Government

Study the '4 fundamentals' on page 44 and Cromwell's observations on the law on page 42, and then answer the following questions:
a) According to the '4 fundamentals', what does Cromwell regard as the basic constitutional requirements in the English state? (4 marks)
b) As described by Cromwell in the extract on page 42, what were the prevailing weaknesses in the legal system? (5 marks)
c) How useful to a historian are these two extracts as illustrations of the governmental problems that faced Oliver Cromwell as Protector? (6 marks)

2 The Rule of the Saints and of the Major-Generals

Study the summons on page 39, the Instructions on page 45, and the comment by Barry Coward on page 46. Answer the following questions:
a) Using your own knowledge and the evidence in the summons, examine the reasoning behind Cromwell's calling of the Nominated Assembly. (7 marks)
b) What evidence can be discerned in the Instructions that might explain the subsequent unpopularity of the Major-Generals? (5 marks)
c) How far does the evidence in the summons and in the Instructions support Coward's contention as expressed in the extract on page 46? (8 marks)

3 Cromwell and Kingship

Read the extracts from Cromwell's conversation on page 50, the army petition on page 51 and Cromwell's address to parliament on page 51.

Answer the following questions:

a) In the light of your own knowledge and the evidence in the extract, explain what you understand the petitioners to mean by the term 'the good old cause'. (5 marks)

b) According to the evidence in the extract on page 50, what was Cromwell's attitude towards monarchy as an institution? (6 marks)

c) How adequate are these extracts as an explanation of Cromwell's reasons for declining the offer of kingship? (6 marks)

d) Using these extracts and your own knowledge, describe the circumstances, and analyse the consequences, of Cromwell's decision not to accept the title of king in 1657. (8 marks)

CHAPTER 4

Cromwell, the Sectaries and the Royalists

In Chapter 3 an examination was made of the attempts during the Protectorate to effect a stable and lasting settlement in England. Emphasis was laid on the political and constitutional developments. This chapter analyses the pressures and tensions which gave shape to the politics of the time and offers an assessment of the role of the central figure in all this, Oliver Cromwell.

1 The Radical Sectaries

Judged by the amount of attention paid to it, the most pressing concern of the day was religion. It was the great issue that defied settlement. What made it so was the religious splintering that had followed in the wake of the civil wars. The challenge to the established Church and the ending of censorship which occurred in the 1640s encouraged the growth of separatist denominations which rejected the idea of a central state church. Ten years had seen a great change. In 1640 there had been two main Protestant Churches: in England, the Anglican with its Arminian and Puritan wings; in Scotland, the Presbyterian with its strongly Calvinist beliefs. In contrast, by the early 1650s, there were scores of separatist sects in existence, none of them willing to conform to the dictates of an established church, Anglican or Presbyterian.

In order to understand why the sects flourished we need to set them in the atmosphere of their time. The upheavals of the 1640s, climaxing with the abolition of monarchy, had created a ferment of ideas, and had convinced many that they were living in a unique period. This conviction was expressed in the 1650s in a widespread belief in 'providence', the concept that events are never random and isolated but are part of a larger divine plan. Cromwell himself had declared: 'The Lord hath done things amongst us as have not been known these thousand years'. For the radical sectaries it was a short step from a belief in providence to an utter conviction that the extraordinary events which had occurred were portents of some great cataclysm. This thought-process is often described as 'millenarianism'. Strictly, the word refers to a particular belief in the imminence of the millennium, the thousand-year period during which Jesus Christ would return to reclaim the earth and govern it with his saints, but the term millenarian is used generally to include all those who believed that a great and revolutionary change in the order of things was about to take place in England.

The extreme forms of millenarianism were deeply disturbing to the civil authorities. It is not difficult to understand why. Those who believed that the end of the world was nigh were very ready to dispense with existing laws and practices. The wilder millenarians asked why they should bother with man-made laws and regulations when God himself was about to sweep all such things away.

Since the sectaries played such an important role during the Interregnum, it is necessary to specify the key ideas and beliefs of the main sects that came into being or into prominence during the English Revolution. These are listed below as the Baptists, the Congregationalists, the Fifth Monarchists, the Muggletonians, the Quakers, the Seekers, and the Shakers. The numbers belonging to each sect are difficult to judge, but they cannot have been large. For example, one modern estimate of the strength of the Baptist movement is that it represented barely one in 400 of the population in the 1650s. However, it was not their numbers that gave the sects significance but the fears that their disruptive notions excited among the governments of the Interregnum.

It is worth stressing that in defining sectarian ideas we very probably give them far more precision than they actually had. Many of the sectaries were inspired as much by emotional impulse as by rationally-determined doctrine. That is why they were so impatient with the traditional type of church organisation and worship which had been based on prescribed theology. It also explains why many of them did not restrict themselves exclusively to membership of one sect. For instance, Laurence Clarkson, who ended up as a Muggletonian, had begun his religious life as an Anglican; in between, he had been variously a Presbyterian, an Independent, a Particular Baptist, a Ranter and a Seeker.

a) Baptists

The Baptist movement, which had begun earlier in the century, became particularly prominent during the 1640s. Its central belief was that faith was a matter of personal experience and acceptance; it could not be taught or learned. Infant baptism was, therefore, meaningless. Great religious value was placed upon the act of adult baptism, usually by total immersion, as an expression of the individual's choosing to become one with Christ. Such a practice and belief involved a direct denial of an organised church with priests or ministers with authority to teach and to administer sacraments.

The movement became divided between 'General' Baptists, those who were willing to co-operate with other sects, and 'Particular' Baptists, those who believed in remaining exclusive. In the 1650s the Baptists aroused marked detestation among religious and political conservatives. This was because the movement was associated, unfairly, with the licence and excess of the notorious Anabaptists of sixteenth-century Munster. In truth, there was little connection between the English and German forms apart from the similarity of name, but in the religious controversies of the mid-seventeenth century such distinctions easily became blurred. Baptists tended to look to Cromwell to protect them, and he certainly did intervene on a number of occasions to prevent their persecution by parliament.

b) Congregationalists (Independents)

It would be misleading to think of congregationalism as a particular denomination. Rather, the term refers broadly to the separatist or independent Protestant congregations who rejected the idea of a national centrally-administered church. It is often used to describe the 'gathered churches', those congregations of godly persons who came together to worship in the spirit of the Lord. This activity often covered a wide range of viewpoints. Since congregationalism did not seek to impose a rigid theology, many former Anglican priests found themselves able to make the transition into congregational pastors.

That Oliver Cromwell was regarded as an Independent is instructive. He was not opposed to church organisation as such but he believed it must be a voluntary association; it ought not to be imposed on believers. In this respect, Cromwell may be viewed as an interesting representative of congregationalism, one of the more moderate religious movements of its time. On a number of occasions, when the extreme sectaries threatened to create religious chaos, the congregationalists closed ranks with the Presbyterians and Anglicans.

c) Fifth Monarchists

The clearest expression of millenarianism was to be found among the Fifth Monarchists. This sect, which never numbered more than 10,000, drew the majority of its members from the army and included officers, chaplains and troopers. Colonel Thomas Harrison became their leading spokesman. They derived their central belief from the book of Revelations in the New Testament and the book of Daniel in the Old. They interpreted these as prophesying that five great monarchies would in turn rule the earth. They believed that the Assyrian, the Persian, the Greek and Roman had been the first four, and that the execution of Charles I had ushered in the fifth and greatest monarchy, the reign of King Jesus. It followed that the government of England should therefore be given over to the rule of the Saints. The Fifth Monarchists' great opportunity seemed to have arrived with the convening of the Nominated Assembly in 1653. However, the subsequent failure of the 'Parliament of the Saints' left them embittered. They turned their anger against Cromwell whom they had hailed earlier as a second Moses. They remained a constant political irritant throughout the Protectorate, challenging his authority and accusing him of thwarting God's purpose on earth.

Indeed, the more fanatical among them posed a real threat to Cromwell; Fifth Monarchists were to be found behind the majority of assassination attempts against him, the most notorious being the plot organised by Thomas Venner in 1657 to murder Cromwell as a prelude to the enforced establishment of the rule of the Saints in England. The crushing of this rising did not mark the end of their efforts. There were further unsuccessful Fifth Monarchist challenges in 1659. Despite the execution of Thomas Harrison as a regicide in 1660, the Fifth Monarchists made one last unavailing attempt under Venner to overthrow the government in 1661.

d) Muggletonians

This sect took its name from Lodowick Muggleton, a London tailor, who believed that Christ had visited him in person and given him the power to save or damn all other men. This was an extension of the predestinarian ideas he had drawn from his earlier Calvinism. The small sect he formed in 1652, made up not surprisingly of those whom he had declared to be saved, saw no need to seek converts. Assured of their own unique virtue, they felt free to reject any state or church laws that impinged upon them. The Muggletonians were far too small a group to represent a serious challenge to the social or political order. Nevertheless their extremist views made them useful bogeymen to be used by the authorities as a warning against the dangers of permitting too much religious toleration.

e) Seekers and Ranters

It is worthwhile considering these two groups together for there was considerable overlap between them. They are both interesting examples of the type of religion that is based upon feelings rather than theology. Their basic conviction was that God manifested Himself not as an external power but as a spiritual force within the individual. Believers should, therefore, 'seek' the divine spirit not in an organised church or even in the Bible but within themselves by responding to their own promptings. The term Ranter derives from the practice of declaiming their thoughts aloud whenever the inspiration took them. What made such groups dangerous in the eyes of the authorities was their flouting of social convention. Ranters tended to live communally with wives and property held in common, which gave opportunity for opponents to condemn them as sexually depraved. It was largely in order to check the activities of the Seekers and Ranters that the Rump introduced the Blasphemy Act of 1650. The importance of these two sects historically lies in the fact that their idea of an inner light or spirit became the essential tenet of the Quakers, the most politically and socially disruptive of the religious movements of the 1650s.

f) Quakers

The most clearly defined rejection of the authority of church and state was to be found in the Quaker movement which began in the early 1650s under the leadership of George Fox and James Nayler and grew by the end of the decade to be over 50,000 strong. The fundamental Quaker belief was that the Lord's message came to individuals directly through the 'inner light' of their own personal inspiration, 'God within them'. Since there was no intermediary between God and man, only the Lord Himself was entitled to obedience. It followed that all earthly authority, whether of church or state, was a corruption and all earthly officials undeserving of respect. Quakers often expressed their beliefs combatively; they frequently disrupted church services by abusing and shouting down the preacher. They were also resolute, as were many other sects, in their refusal to pay tithes, the traditional local tax levied for the upkeep of the parish clergy. It is easy to see why contemporaries regarded the Quakers as among the most socially dangerous of the radical groups.

The prayer meetings of the 'Society of Friends' took the form of individual believers speaking out their thoughts as the Lord inspired them. This invariably involved much physical quaking, hence their title. Such a pattern of worship was obviously open to abuse by the neurotic or those in love with the sound of their own voice, but in practice Quaker meetings seem to have been remarkably harmonious. There was sufficient shared belief to allow such expressions of inspiration on the part of the individual to be accepted by the whole assembly.

It is interesting that the modern Quaker movement should now be strongly identified with pacifism. In the 1650s it was seen as a disruptive organisation quite prepared to use force when it felt threatened. This may well be the reason why the court lists of the time show so many prosecutions of Quakers and why the magistrates frequently gave Quaker offenders severe sentences. Over 2,000 Quakers were brought to trial during the Interregnum. The distinctive style of their speech and dress frequently aroused considerable opposition in the localities. Their refusal to conform to the custom of doffing their hats as a mark of respect, even when brought before magistrates or judges, was hardly calculated to endear them to the civil authorities, who often turned a blind eye when Quakers were set upon, as they frequently were, by the local rowdies.

Cromwell was not opposed to the Quakers over their form of worship; his worry, as with all the religious sects, was not their private beliefs but their public behaviour. If they engaged in disruptive or scandalous practices, this could only delay the process of healing and settling. He was on good personal terms with George Fox, and interceded on occasion to prevent Quakers from being prosecuted without good reason. The notable example of this was his reaction to the notorious case of James Nayler in 1656. In October of that year Nayler had ridden into Bristol on a donkey, surrounded by adoring women, in apparent imitation of Christ's entry into Jerusalem on the first Palm Sunday. He was arrested for blasphemy by local magistrates. Fears of widespread Quaker disturbances led to what was in itself a minor local affair being taken up by parliament, which ordered Nayler to be brought to Westminster. In self-righteous zeal, the House denounced Nayler and sentenced him to a series of brutal punishments, which included a ferocious flogging and the boring through of his tongue.

Cromwell was deeply disturbed, not simply by the the savagery of Nayler's treatment, but because he believed parliament had exceeded its authority. In December he wrote sharply to the Speaker to inform parliament that nothing in the *Instrument of Government* conferred on them the legal powers they had claimed. His chief anxiety was that parliament had gone beyond its constitutional rights by denying 'liberty of conscience'.

2 Cromwell and the Sects

Religious considerations weighed heavily with Cromwell, both because of the intensity of his own spiritual convictions, and because he believed that the root cause of the civil wars had been religious division. When, as Protector, Cromwell spoke of 'healing and settling' he was referring to the need to establish religious harmony in England. It was the essential part of his idea of national 'godliness'; his conviction was that the turmoil of the civil wars had been God's way of preparing England for religious peace, which it was now the duty of those in government to achieve.

Cromwell condemned those religious fanatics who 'press their finger upon their brethren's conscience'. His view was typically and clearly expressed in his defence of a soldier, named Packer, who had been cashiered because of his religious views. Cromwell wrote to Packer's commanding officer, Major-General Crawford, a Presbyterian:

1 The man is an Anabaptist ... Admit he be, shall that render him incapable to serve the Public? He is indiscreet. It may be so; in some things, we have all human infirmities. I tell you, if you had none but such indiscreet men about you, and would be pleased to
5 use them kindly, you would find [them] as good a fence to you as any you have yet chosen. Sir, the State, in choosing men to serve them, takes no notice of their opinions; if they be willing faithfully to serve them, that satisfies. I advised you formerly to bear with

men of different minds from yourself. Take heed of being sharp, or
10 too easily sharpened by others, against those to whom you can
object little but that they square not with you in every opinion
concerning matters of religion.

Cromwell believed that religious freedom was a fundamental right, but
he was very conscious of the difficulty in bringing the various sects to
recognise each other's freedoms.

Liberty of conscience is a natural right; and he that would have it,
ought to give it. Indeed that hath been one of the vanities of our
contests. Every sect saith: 'Oh, give me liberty!' but give him it, and
he will not yield it to anybody else.

He frequently expressed his dismay that those very people who had
joined the struggle against Charles I in order to gain religious freedom
for themselves were now denying it to others:

1 Those that were sound in the faith, how proper was it for them to
labour for liberty, for a just liberty, that men should not be
trampled upon for their consciences! Had not they laboured, but
lately, under the weight of persecutions? And was it fit for them to
5 sit heavy upon others? Is it ingenuous to ask liberty, and not to give
it? What greater hypocrisy than for those who were oppressed by
the Bishops to become the greatest oppressors themselves, so soon
as their yoke was removed.

Cromwell held that unless a particular religious belief led to subversive
public behaviour it should be tolerated.

1 Our practice hath been, to let all this Nation see that whatever
pretensions to religion would continue quiet, peaceable, they
should enjoy conscience and liberty to themselves; - and not make
Religion a pretence for arms and blood; truly we have suffered
5 them, and that cheerfully, so to enjoy their own liberties. If a man
of one form will be trampling upon the heels of another man; if an
Independent, for example, will despise him who is under Baptism
and will revile him and reproach and provoke him, I will not suffer
it in him. If, on the other side, those of the Baptists shall be
10 censuring the godly ministers of the nation that profess under that
of Independency; or those that profess under Presbytery shall be
reproaching or speaking ill of them, slandering them and censuring
them - as I would not be willing to see the day on which England
shall be in the power of Presbytery to impose upon the consciences
15 of others that profess faith in Christ - so I will not endure to
reproach them. God give us hearts and spirits to keep them equal.

Cromwell's advocacy of toleration was not simply a matter of words. He took practical steps to achieve it. Among the ordinances of 1653 (see page 42) were two notable measures which aimed to bring order to the disputed question of church appointments. The title of the ordinances gave a clear indication of their purpose: 'An Ordinance for Appointing Commissioners for Approbation of Public Preachers' and 'An Ordinance for Ejecting Scandalous, Ignorant and Insufficient Ministers and Schoolmasters'. Between them the Ordinances set up a body of Commissioners, subsequently known as 'Triers and Ejectors', who were responsible for the selection and the supervision of those appointed to public ministries in the Church. Significantly, the ordinances made no attempt to prescribe what doctrines were acceptable. Cromwell's aim was not to persecute particular beliefs but, on the contrary, to provide greater toleration by removing or debarring those clerics whose extreme views or behaviour disturbed the religious peace for which he longed. He was anxious that the Commissioners should be drawn from as many denominations as possible; Baptists, Independents, and Presbyterians appeared in the lists of appointees. The evidence suggests that his policy was largely successful. Even some of the strongest critics of Cromwell's religious toleration admitted that the work of the Triers and Ejectors did improve the quality of the church ministry. Moreover, in practice, relatively few of the incumbent ministers needed to be removed, since the great majority showed themselves ready to reform and improve their behaviour.

Cromwell was engaged in a balancing act throughout the Protectorate, trying to satisfy the army, whose natural sympathies were with the sects, without alienating parliament which became increasingly dominated by conservative Presbyterians as the 1650s wore on. At the same time, he still had hopes of achieving a religious settlement that would provide the conditions of godliness and allow toleration while not permitting the extremists to impose themselves. During his Protectorate Cromwell made considerable efforts to ensure that the parochial system was maintained and improved. This was because he judged that in the conditions of the 1650s the traditional church structure in the localities had to be preserved if the ordinary people were to have access to the means of worship. This also meant the continuation of tithes for the support of the clergy.

Cromwell's attempt at religious balance did not bring him unqualified admiration. His dilemma was that he was invariably more tolerant than were his parliaments. As the Nayler case showed, his efforts to hold parliament's repressive tendencies in check were not always successful. He knew that he was engaged in a thankless task:

1 I have had buffets and rebukes, on the one hand and on the other; some censuring me for Presbytery; others as an encourager of all the sects and heresies in the nation. I have borne my reproach; but

I have through God's mercy not been unhappy in preventing any
5 one religion impose upon another.

His apparent indulgence of the sects worried the more conservative
elements in society. He was referred to mockingly as 'the darling of the
sectaries'. One of the most insistent themes in the huge volume of
pamphlets published in the 1650s was the need to guard against the
threat posed by the religious sectaries. The growing readiness in the late
1650s of the Presbyterians to consider making common cause with the
royalists (see page 92) arose not from any great love for Charles II but
from a fear of what uncontrolled sectarianism might do. A return to
some form of strong, centrally-controlled, church authority seemed to
offer the best means of uniting against the religious extremists.

Cromwell belonged to an age of religious intensity that is largely alien
to modern Western thought. In some respects, as in his treatment of
Ireland, he appears repellently bigoted. But Ireland is the great
exception. It is arguable that, judged by the standards of the age in which
he lived, he was the most tolerant of rulers. Cromwell was the first
English statesman to make religious toleration the basis of government
policy. This needs to be put in its mid-seventeenth century context. He
was not a modern liberal. His toleration was selective and conditional. It
did not extend, for example, to Catholicism or what he called
'blasphemy', by which he meant the extreme sectaries. Nevertheless, it is
arguable that under Cromwell's Protectorate, England experienced an
unprecedented degree of religious freedom.

3 Cromwell and the Royalists

One of Cromwell's consistent fears as Protector was that the unsettled
situation might encourage a royalist reaction in England. Much of his
foreign policy was directed at preventing the Stuarts from finding allies
abroad willing to support such a venture. His anxieties are
understandable, but with hindsight it can be seen that they were
exaggerated. The royalists themselves represented only a minor threat to
the Protectorate. It was only when the other conservative forces in
England allied with them, something which did not happen until after
Cromwell's death, that the restoration of the Stuart monarchy became a
possibility.

Following his defeat at the Battle of Worcester in 1651, Charles II
fled to the Continent where he remained for the next nine years. His
enforced absence left the royalists leaderless and made it very difficult
for them to organise themselves into an effective opposition to the
republican regimes of the Interregnum. Until 1658 the strength and
reputation of Cromwell's army made thoughts of a successful royalist
rising unrealistic. Moreover, there was little support in the localities for
the royalist cause; while few people were enthusiastic supporters of the

Commonwealth and the Protectorate, they were not willing to put themselves at risk by openly challenging those in power. Most royalists were cowed by the restrictions that branded them as 'delinquents', imposing heavy fines on them and in some cases making their estates forfeit. The introduction by the Major-Generals of a further 'decimation' tax on royalists was largely successful in its aim of convincing them that open expressions of support for the Stuarts carried too high a price. It is now acknowledged that the Sealed Knot, the royalist organisation supposedly concerned with planning a Stuart restoration, spent most of its time discouraging risings because it feared that their almost inevitable failure would discredit the royalist cause.

The one exception to the pattern was the rising led by John Penruddock in Wiltshire in 1655. It began as an attempt on the part of some royalists in exile to prove that their cause was still alive. Believing that there were potential centres of resistance throughout the country just waiting to be a given a lead, they encouraged Penruddock, a former royalist Colonel, to seize Salisbury, an important administrative centre in the west country. Penruddock duly led a contingent of royalist troops, variously estimated at between 200 and 400, in an attack upon the gaol in Salisbury. The information on which the exiles had based their plans proved woefully inaccurate. Penruddock's attack aroused practically no support either locally or nationally. After only two days his force was scattered and defeated. Penruddock and the leading conspirators were tried and executed, while a number of the lesser rebels were transported to the Barbadoes.

As significant as the rising itself was the speed with which Cromwell's government responded to put it down. Equally striking was the readiness with which the authorities in the localities reacted, and their ability to raise some 4,000 local militia troops to crush the rising. This indicates that, although there might well have been considerable latent sympathy for the idea of a return to monarchy, there were few in 1655 willing to put their lives or livelihood at risk by openly supporting royalist ventures. This illustrates a characteristic of the whole period 1640-60 on which modern historians lay great stress - the tendency of great majority of the population towards neutrality. Their natural inclination was to avoid trouble. Sometimes, against their will, they were drawn by circumstances into affairs which obliged them to take sides, but their choice was frequently more a matter of expediency than of conviction.

Another factor that undermined Penruddock's venture was the quality of the intelligence service on which the government were able to rely. This contrasted sharply with the inadequacy of the royalists' network of communication. Credit for this lies with John Thurloe, Cromwell's Secretary of State. In the tradition of Elizabeth I's great spy master, Walsingham, Thurloe operated an elaborate espionage system. A constant stream of reports from informers and double agents in

Europe as well as England allowed him to be always one step ahead of those plotting against the Protectorate. The famous diarist, Samuel Pepys, remarking on the success of Thurloe's spy system, wrote: 'Cromwell carried the secrets of all the princes of Europe at his girdle'. Thurloe's prior knowledge of the royalists' plans helps to explain the speed and effectiveness with which Penruddock's Rising was suppressed.

A genuine challenge to the regimes of the Protectorate required an organised coalition of all the forces opposed to it. Given the strength of the army, this had little chance of occurring until after Cromwell's death. The key to the survival of the Commonwealth and Protectorate was the loyalty of the army. Although on occasion factions within the armed forces expressed deep dissatisfaction with the governments and parliaments of the 1650s, Cromwell never seriously looked liked losing the loyalty of the troops under him. His successes as a commander since 1642 and his readiness to take up the grievances of his troops had endeared him to the army. Affection for him personally and respect for his reputation survived throughout the 1650s. However, the situation changed once his strong hand was removed. The precarious stability that Cromwell had been able to preserve broke down. Faction returned and the struggle over who controlled the executive was renewed.

4 Cromwell as Protector

Cromwell was in a paradoxical position as Protector. He was heir to a revolution but he was not a revolutionary. In all that he did as Protector he favoured traditional forms. His basic political approach was one of caution. This is well illustrated by his rejection of the offer of the Crown, even though he believed that the best system for England was one that had 'something monarchical in it'. He always sought to work within the constitution as he understood it; he accepted the *Instrument of Government* and the *Humble Petition and Advice,* which placed him under certain constraints. He depended on military power, but was reluctant to use it to impose himself on the nation as a dictator. He occupied a halfway position. Having been instrumental in removing the Stuart monarchy, he was then unwilling to go further and create an entirely new system. Although on occasion he used force, as in his dissolution of the Rump, it was always as a last resort. When faced by the widespread unpopularity created by the system of Major-Generals, he allowed the experiment to be abandoned.

In a sense Cromwell's position as Protector meant that he got the worst of both worlds. On the one hand, he lacked the authority and public acceptance associated with traditional monarchy; on the other, he never pushed his authority to the point where he had a genuine controlling power. What added to the ambiguity of his position was that as Protector he was the hope of many who had supported the parliamentary cause since 1642 in order to create a new order in church and state. Cromwell's disinclination to follow a radical path when in office deeply disappointed them. He was accused of being both a hypocrite and a turn-coat.

'He doth smile and smile even while he smites thee under the fifth rib.' So said a Leveller pamphlet in 1649 by way of illustrating Cromwell's treachery and hypocrisy. To those, such as the Levellers and republicans, who found Cromwell's government to be a tyranny both in concept and practice, clearly his hypocrisy was self-evident. However, to those who understood the difficulties in which Cromwell found himself as Lord Protector, trying to exercise balanced yet effective authority, the charge of hypocrisy did not stand. They saw him as being faced with insuperable problems in a time of uncertainty, discord and unresolved constitutional questions.

What needs to be considered is that Cromwell was so involved with the everyday running of government that he had little time to develop an overall policy. Historians in the past have sometimes overlooked such constraints and have ascribed too much purpose and planning to his exercise of office. It is doubtful whether Cromwell really knew his own intentions very far ahead. He was essentially an opportunist, who justified his actions after the event by reference to the Lord's divine will. He is recorded as having said that, 'He climbs not so high as he who knows not wither he goeth'. Gerald Aylmer sums him up neatly as 'a pragmatist who waited on providence'.

Of course, Cromwell did have broad aims. He wanted a godly commonwealth and a 'reformation of manners', by which he meant that in public and private affairs moral considerations should govern behaviour. In social terms, he was very much a conservative. He wanted the traditional stratified class structure to remain: 'a nobility, a gentry and a yeomanry - that is a good estate', he observed. In religion, he appealed for what he called 'liberty for tender consciences', the right of individuals, provided they were not Papists or blasphemers, to worship God as they saw fit without having to conform to the dictates of an organised church.

However, it is the broadness of these aims that is most notable. He seldom translated them into clear and specific programmes. Most of his time as Lord Protector was spent in trying to control the excessive demands of others. His dissolutions of parliament were usually on the grounds that it had exceeded its authority or was making demands that threatened the balance on which order depended. He could not, however, escape the dilemma that accompanied his position. He was Protector because he was head of the army. Try as he might to restore effective civilian government, his authority was basically military. Yet given the power he held, he was very sparing in its use. In a number of remarkable respects Oliver Cromwell's personal rule was the opposite of tyranny. He tried to make parliament representative, and to give it a genuine role in the constitution. This is an aspect greatly stressed by modern scholars. Aylmer observes: 'If this was a military dictatorship it was a reluctant and exceptionally legalistic one'.

Nonetheless, the fact remains that in the final analysis Cromwell was, in Christopher Hill's graphic words, 'sitting on bayonets and nothing else'. No matter how genuinely fair-minded and tolerant his policies were, he was in a position to introduce them only because of the power he wielded, by virtue of his military strength. He may have been reluctant to use force, but this could not disguise the fact that he retained the power to do so. As Derek Hirst has remarked of him: 'Sheathing the sword was not the same thing as laying it down'.

---

the radical sects defined

Baptists Independents Congregationalists Fifth Monarchists
Muggletonians Seekers Ranters Quakers

their threat to the traditional order in church and state

Cromwell's religious attitudes

his relations with the sects   his wish to establish godly government
his belief in liberty of conscience

---

the royalists during the Protectorate

Penruddock's Rising, 1655

Cromwell as Protector

his relations with the army his political and religious enemies
the limits of his authority
the extent of his achievements

Summary - Cromwell, the Sectaries and the Royalists

Making notes on '*Cromwell, the Sectaries and the Royalists*'

This chapter has four main themes: the radical sectaries, Cromwell's relations with them, the royalist threat during the Protectorate, and an assessment of Cromwell as Protector. The following selection of key points with accompanying questions will provide a useful framework against which to test your understanding of the material.

1 The Sects -
   Why had they become so prominent by the early 1650s?
   Identify the chief characteristics of the Baptists, the Congregationalists, the Fifth Monarchists, the Muggletonians, the Quakers, the Seekers, and the Shakers.

2 Cromwell and the Sects -
   His concept of 'liberty of conscience'.
   How did he distinguish between the sects on religious and political grounds? Was he the 'darling of the sectaries'?

3 Cromwell and the Royalists -
   The morale of the royalists after Worcester.
   Why did Penruddock's Rising occur? Why did it fail?

4 Cromwell as Protector -
   His approach to government. How dependent was he on the army?
   His objectives? How clear-cut were they?
   The pressures on him as Protector - Who were the enemies of the Protectorate?
   The nature of his authority - Was Cromwell a dictator?

Answering essay questions on '*Cromwell, the Sectaries and the Royalists*'

It is unlikely that exam questions would be set directly on the sects themselves. What is more probable is that you would be asked to analyse some aspect of Cromwell's relations with them. Consider the following:

1 To what extent was the character of the Protectorate shaped by Cromwell's objective of achieving 'a godly nation'?
2 How appropriate is the description of Cromwell as 'the darling of the sectaries'?
3 What light does Cromwell's relations with the radical sectaries throw upon the problems he confronted as Protector?

Questions 2 and 3 are obviously closely related in regard to subject matter. In each case what is called for is an analysis of the constraints that Cromwell put upon himself by his attempts to extend toleration to the sects. His balanced approach to government is clearly a crucial factor. The weighting in question 1 is more on Cromwell's own spiritual beliefs. Appropriate reference to his understanding of what 'godliness' constituted is essential here.

Examiners remain fond of the royalists as a theme. Invariably, given the subject matter, they concentrate on the aspect of failure. Typical questions are:

4   Why were the supporters of the Stuarts unable to mount an effective resistance to the Cromwellian Protectorate?

5   'Unrealistic in conception, inept in practice': How accurate is this as an explanation of the failure of Penruddock's Rising (1655)?

6   Consider the assertion that 'the failure of the royalist cause in the 1650s was a matter not of Protectorate strength but of royalist weakness'.

You will notice that Penruddock's Rising, even when not specified, is central to each of these questions. This is because it was the only major overt challenge to the Protectorate. Consequently, an analysis of the reasons for its failure provides the essential material for all the questions.

Oliver Cromwell as Protector is obviously a major examination topic area. The questions below touch on some central themes:

7   Were the problems confronting Oliver Cromwell as Protector predominantly political or religious?

8   How accurate is it to suggest that, as Protector, Oliver Cromwell was 'King in all but name'?

9   Examine the view that Cromwell's difficulties as Protector arose from his reluctance to use the power that he had at his disposal.

In order to allow yourself a full coverage you may well care to refer to the the political and constitutional analysis in Chapter 3 and the foreign policy material in Chapter 5. Central to each of the answers is an analysis of Cromwell's objectives as Protector. Was his essential aim one of balance? Did he try to play off the political and religious groups against each other? What powers did he actually have at his command? Were there any limitations on that power? The material you compile from such supplementary questions can then be used to good effect in tackling the specified questions.

***Source-based questions on** 'Cromwell, the Sectaries and the Royalists'*

1 Cromwell and Liberty of Conscience

Study Cromwell's defence of Packer, the Anabaptist, on pages 63-4, and his comments on page 64. Answer the following questions:

a) Examine the significance of the following statements as made by Cromwell:
'the State, in choosing men to serve them, takes no notice of their opinions' (page 63 lines 6-7). (5 marks)
'Liberty of conscience is a natural right' (page 64). (5 marks)
'men should not be trampled upon for their consciences' (page 64). (5 marks)
b) Using your own knowledge and the material in the sources, explain why Cromwell was so concerned with the question of religious liberty during his Protectorate. (7 marks)
c) How adequate a picture of Cromwell's attitude towards the sects do these sources provide? (8 marks)

2 Cromwell and the Sects
Study Cromwell's statements on page 64, and then answer the following questions:
a) What religious ideas do you associate with the following groups to which Cromwell makes reference: 'the Baptists' (5 marks) 'Independency' (5 marks) 'Presbytery'? (5 marks)
b) How justified would you judge Cromwell to be in accusing the sects of 'hypocrisy'? For what reasons might he have been particularly sensitive on this issue? (7 marks)
c) How consistently in practice did Cromwell apply the principle of freedom for the sects which he defines in these sources? (8 marks)

CHAPTER 5

Foreign Policy During the Interregnum

1 Background

The Reformation, which had begun in the reign of Henry VIII and had been consolidated under Elizabeth I, had made England a Protestant nation. This put her at variance with the Catholic states of Europe, the two most powerful being Spain and France. Spain was viewed as the greater menace, since her Habsburg rulers saw it as their religious duty to lead a holy crusade against such 'apostate' countries as England. There were deep fears among European Protestants that Spain was intent on becoming 'a universal monarchy', for besides being a leading power in Europe she had also acquired a great overseas empire by conquering large areas in the newly-discovered Americas. The terrors that Spain aroused in the sixteenth and seventeenth centuries may be compared to the anxieties felt by the West about Soviet expansionism during the Cold War period of the twentieth century.

The unsuccessful attempt of the Armada to invade England in 1588 was the outstanding example of Anglo-Spanish hostility. Ever after, distrust of Spain remained a dominant English attitude, particularly among Puritans. They urged that the nation should forge a Protestant alliance against Spain. Little came of this during the reigns of the first two Stuarts, since both James I and Charles I chose to avoid foreign entanglements where possible. This angered those Puritan critics who regarded the Stuarts' reluctance to become involved in a Protestant league as evidence of their sympathy with popery. Such bitterness underlay much of the criticism voiced in parliament of royal foreign policy.

Between 1641 and 1648 there had been frequent rumours of royalist plans to bring French or Spanish forces into England to crush parliament, but none of these had materialised. No foreign country played a direct part in the English civil wars. One reason was that Europe was largely preoccupied with the last stages of the Thirty Years War, which occurred between 1618 and 1648. Initially, this had been a struggle between Catholic and Protestant states but as the war progressed it became increasingly difficult to define it as a religious conflict. National rather than religious considerations seemed to determine the actions of the states involved. This became particularly evident from 1635 onwards when the two major Catholic powers, Spain and France, went to war against each other. It was this blurring of the religious issue that confounded the hopes of those English Puritans who expected that with the abolition of kingship English foreign policy would become distinctly Protestant again.

The reason why foreign alignments could not be formed simply along denominational lines was that concerns other than religion had begun to shape national attitudes. Foremost among these was economics. For more than a century trade rivalry had been a cause of growing hostility between England and other continental countries. Where religious division and commercial rivalry coincided, as was the case with England and Spain, mutual antagonism was the logical and obvious result. But it was seldom as simple as that. Religious sympathies and commercial interests did not always match. This was particularly the case with England and Holland (the United Provinces of the Netherlands). As far as religion was concerned, the two countries shared a common Protestantism. However, this did not create a harmony of interest. Their trade rivalry in Europe and the East Indies and their long-running dispute over fishing grounds tended to take precedence over their religious sympathies. This became especially evident with the ending of the Thirty Years War in 1648, which had the disturbing result for England of leaving the large Dutch merchant fleet free to monopolise the shipping routes in the North Sea and the Baltic.

2 The Commonwealth and External Affairs

The execution of Charles I in January 1649 caused a deep sense of shock in all the European courts, Catholic and Protestant. For a time this created hopes among royalists and fears among republicans that there would be pro-Stuart foreign interventions in England. However, Cromwell's subjugation of Ireland and Scotland removed the immediate threat of a successful royalist reaction and enabled the Rump to consider what its attitude should be to the outside world.

One of its first thoughts was that it could strengthen its position internationally by an agreement with the United Provinces. Superficially there seemed to be very good reasons why England and Holland should come together. They were both Protestant, both had a strong anti-Spanish tradition, and they had both very recently become republics. Accordingly, the Rump, expecting that their representatives would be be warmly received, sent a special mission to the Hague to discuss the terms of an alliance. However, what the new English government had not grasped was the degree of anger aroused by the recent execution of Charles I. Although Holland was predominantly republican in its outlook, the other provinces still contained a strong sympathy for the House of Orange, which until 1650 had ruled over the Netherlands. The execution in England of the reigning monarch appeared to have deeply disturbed them. When the English ambassadors arrived in the Dutch capital they were subjected to insults and shouts of 'regicides' from the crowds in the streets. Not surprisingly, the mission ended in failure.

a) The Navigation Act, 1651

In his report back to the Rump, the leading ambassador, Oliver St.John, roundly condemned the Dutch for abandoning the Protestant cause and for being concerned solely with their own self-interest. He described them as 'juggling sharks'. St.John became the chief mover of the Navigation Act, which the Rump then introduced as a way of punishing the Dutch for their refusal to enter into an alliance. There was a further and, arguably, a much stronger motive in that the merchant-dominated Rump was eager to strike a blow against the United Provinces as England's major commercial rival.

The Navigation Act, which was introduced in 1650 and finally passed in October 1651, laid down that all goods imported into Britain from Africa, Asia or the Americas were to be carried only in British vessels, and that exports from Europe were to be admitted into Britain only in British ships or those of the exporting country. This is often referred to as an early example of mercantilism, a form of protection or trade war. The introduction of the Navigation Act was accompanied by the deliberate whipping up of anti-Dutch hysteria. The Rump encouraged the publication of cheap newspapers and broadsheets depicting the Dutch as renegade Protestants, still besotted with monarchy, and corrupted by thoughts of commercial gain. The Dutch retaliated angrily by denouncing what they regarded as English fanaticism and hypocrisy. Open war between the countries became increasingly likely. It needed only a pretext.

b) The Dutch War, 1652-4

This duly came in May 1652 when the Dutch and English fleets encountered each other in the Downs, off the Kent coast. Defying a demand that they respect the English republican flag by lowering their own flags in deference, the Dutch opened fire instead. The war that ensued lasted until April 1654. It took the form of a series of naval engagements, fought mainly in the Channel and North-Sea areas. Initially the Dutch, led by Admiral Van Tromp, had the better of affairs but with his death in the Battle of Texel in August 1653 the war turned against them. The emergence of Robert Blake as a naval commander of genius began to give the English a distinct advantage. It was also at this juncture that the Rump government began to derive great benefit from the strengthening of the navy that had been initiated by Charles I. It was a bitter irony for the royalists to have to contemplate.

A series of English victories led to the blockading of the Dutch coast. By December 1653 the Dutch had suffered heavy shipping losses and were willing to cease hostilities. Both sides had good reason at this point for ending the fighting. In Holland, the republicans, under the leadership of John De Witt, had gained the upper hand over the

Orangists, the Dutch royalist party. There was now an unwillingness among the majority of Netherlanders to continue a ruinous war which, at least in part, was being fought on behalf of the Stuarts. December 1653 also marked a significant political change in England. With the resignation of the Nominated Assembly, whose religious fanatics had been passionately committed to war against the Dutch as betrayers of the Protestant cause, cooler heads began to prevail. Within days of the establishing of the Protectorate peace talks had begun.

3 Foreign Policy under the Protectorate

a) The End of the Dutch War

Cromwell had been a reluctant supporter of war against the Dutch. He regarded it as a scandal that Englishmen should be fighting fellow-Protestants. His abiding conviction was that Spain was the great threat. He was fond of remarking that 'the Spaniard is your natural enemy'. Cromwell believed that he was singled out by God to fight the forces of Anti-Christ, whom he identified in Europe as the Spanish. One way to achieve this would be to unite the Protestant nations of Europe in a godly federation. His belief that he had a divine mission to chastise Spain was an extension of his conviction that he was God's instrument for achieving a reformation of manners in England.

Newly installed as Lord Protector in December 1653, Cromwell was ideally positioned to respond to the growing desire for peace with the United Provinces. He was aided by the timely revelation that the war had been brought about by the machinations of Spain. It was alleged by Puritan propagandists that Jesuit agents in Holland and England had plotted together to create enmity between the two nations as a means of advancing the universal monarchy of Spain. Pamphlets poured forth claiming to show evidence of the treachery. The striking feature of all this was not the concocted evidence itself but the readiness with which it was believed. Cromwell himself claimed to have personal knowledge of Spanish intrigue in the English army.

The purported revelations gave impetus to the peace talks that ended the Anglo-Dutch war. They bore fruit in the Treaty of Westminster in April 1654. The Dutch agreed to abide by the Navigation Act, to honour the English flag at sea, and to cease to offer haven to English royalists. Complaints were voiced in England that the Protector had failed to gain any significant economic advantages from the Treaty. The complaints had substance, for Cromwell at this stage was much more concerned with promoting an anti-Spanish alliance with the Dutch than with enforcing harsh economic terms on them. He was even prepared, as a *quid pro quo*, to offer the Dutch a monopoly of the East India trade if they would make war on Spain. In the event, the Dutch, although sympathetic to Cromwell's plan, were not yet ready for another war and declined to engage themselves against the Spanish.

b) The Western Design and War against Spain

The defeat of the United Provinces greatly enhanced the military reputation of the Protectorate. This encouraged other European nations to consider the advantages of alliance with England. By the end of 1654 the Protectorate had entered into trade agreements with Sweden, Denmark and Portugal. Such agreements strengthened Cromwell in his determination to challenge the power of Spain. The theatre chosen for hostilities was not Europe but the Spanish colonies in the Americas, hence the later description of it as 'the Western Design'. The essential aim was to capture the Caribbean islands from Spain and then turn them into permanent bases from which the English could destroy Spanish shipping and thus break her empire.

The decision to attack Spain was taken in the weeks immediately following the end of the Dutch war. There was no particular provocation to justify the attack but there was a particular opportunity. With the close of the war against Holland, England had at its disposal over 150 war ships and their crews. In session with his Council of State, Cromwell discussed the feasibility of using this formidable force to seize the Spanish colonies. Unfortunately for historians, only a portion of the minutes of this Council meeting have survived, and this has raised doubts about what actually took place. One reading of the evidence is that Cromwell took the initiative in urging the Council to make war as a form of crusade. He denounced the King of Spain as 'the greatest enemy to the Protestant cause in the world' and argued that England had every right to retaliate for the wrongs done to her people. As he later declared to parliament:

1 There is no intelligent person but will easily see how empty and weak the reasons are that the Spaniard has for claiming for himself alone an empire of such vast and prodigious extent. The Spaniards endeavour to justify themselves for having enslaved, hanged,
5 drowned, tortured and put to death our countrymen, robbed them of their ships and goods even in time of profound peace and that without any injury received on their part, which cruel usage and havoc as often as the English call to remembrance they cannot miss to think their former glory is quite gone and their ships of war
10 become entirely useless if they suffer themselves to be any longer treated in such a disgraceful manner.

Another interpretation is that Cromwell, rather than leading the Council to its decision, was persuaded by the merchant representatives to adopt a war policy. One complication is that, although for the sake of convenience it is customary to speak of the merchants as if they were one class of opinion, the truth is that they represented a range of attitudes. There were, for example, merchants who stood to gain greatly from the English seizure of Spain's territories and the takeover of her trade, while there were others, such as the wool merchants, who, because they traded directly with Spain, were unhappy at the prospect of a war involving disruptive embargoes and blockades. It may be that in deference to this latter group, the decision was made to restrict the war to an attack upon the Spanish colonies and to leave European Spain untouched. There are also strong hints that the Council was not unanimous in its decision. John Lambert, for one, appears to have expressed serious doubts about the proposed strategy.

As with the Dutch war, the prelude to hostilities against Spain was a full-scale propaganda campaign. The enemy was depicted as a ravening beast, intent on destroying Protestant liberties throughout Europe, and imposing the tyranny of the Spanish monarchy over the whole world. A torrent of illustrated pamphlets invoked folk memories of the Armada and the Inquisition.

Indeed, greater planning seems to have gone into preparing public opinion for the war than into the actual attack on the Spanish colonies. The broad strategy was clear enough. The large fleet that set sail in December 1654, commanded by William Penn and Robert Venables, aimed to capture the main Spanish-occupied islands in the Caribbean, Hispaniola (modern Haiti) being the principal target. However, the tactics adopted were not well-thought out. The wrong area of the island was chosen for landing, distances were miscalculated, and the troops were decimated by a combination of extreme heat and disease. Moreover, Spanish resistance proved determined and effective. The English withdrew and, very much as an afterthought, re-directed their forces into what proved to be a successful attack upon Jamaica.

Subsequent history was to show that, strategically and economically, the island of Jamaica was as valuable a prize as Hispaniola would have been. Its capture could be said, therefore, to have fulfilled the main purpose of the Western Design. At the time, however, it was difficult to avoid the conclusion that the campaign had been largely a failure. Thousands of troops had been lost and, as many merchants had feared, Spain had retaliated to the unprovoked attack on her colonies by closing her European ports to English vessels. The Dutch were prompt to recoup their recent war losses by moving into the trading areas now barred to the English. Furthermore, with the English fleet preoccupied in the Caribbean, piracy, which was an ever-present menace in this period, had a free hand elsewhere. Above all, the campaign was expensive. At a time when the Protectorate was experiencing severe financial problems, the wasteful expenditure on a dubious Spanish war was difficult to justify.

'The Black Legend of Spain', an English print of 1654

c) Reactions to the Western Design

Initially, Cromwell was deeply depressed by the English failure to take Hispaniola but characteristically he came to terms with it by ascribing it to 'the hand of God'. He interpreted the affair as the Almighty's way of rebuking the English nation for its slowness in adopting true godliness. Besides explaining the failure, this interpretation provided an added justification for his introduction later in 1655 of the rule of the Major-Generals (see page 44).

Cromwell found himself the subject of fierce criticism over the war. One charge was that in his religious zeal he had misunderstood the nature of 'universal monarchy', the main threat of which came, some said, not from Spain but from France. Henry Vane spoke of France as being governed by 'the most tyrannical principles' and being intent upon European domination. Others saw the greater danger coming from Sweden, which, under its powerful monarch, Charles X, had made substantial advances in the Baltic, an area of rapidly expanding commercial importance. One important voice was that of Slingsby Bethel, who believed that Sweden and France represented a joint threat: 'These two countries are like to have divided the Western Empire [by which he meant western Europe] between them'.

Some critics complained that the war had disrupted their trade with Spain. They did not see it as a necessary struggle since Spain was no longer a real power in Europe. They argued that she was a 'lost nation', meaning that her greatness was a thing of the past. We need to appreciate the nature of the commercial objections to the war with Spain. The question of cost was critical. Few were willing to pay the heavy taxes required by the war when the commercial outcome for themselves was loss rather than gain. The Western Design appeared to be pursuing unrealistic religious ends at the expense of hard-headed commercial ones.

d) Cromwell's Colonial Policy

Whatever the validity of these contemporary criticisms, it is now a matter of some controversy whether Cromwell's Western Design constituted an early form of imperialism. Those who think that it did so point to the acquisition and settling of colonies and bases from which a trading empire could be spread. Alan Smith goes so far as to describe Cromwell as the founder of the British Empire. He bases his judgement on evidence such as the active support that Cromwell gave to English Puritan colonists in North America, with whom he had a natural religious sympathy, to expand into neighbouring regions belonging to Holland and France. One example was his sending in 1654 of a naval squadron to seize Acadia (modern Nova Scotia) from the French.

It was also the case that he was anxious to encourage English emigration to the West Indian islands. After Jamaica was acquired in 1655 it was official Protectorate policy to promote settlement there. Assisted passages and guaranteed land rights were offered as inducement.

1 Those that transport themselves ... shall have land let forth unto them, according to the proportion of twenty acres, besides lakes and rivers, for every male of twelve years old and upwards, and ten acres for every other male or female, in some convenient place of
5 the said Island; and in case any whole Plantation, that is to say, the governors and greater part of the people shall remove themselves, they shall be preferred in respect of the place of their setting down, that it may be near some good harbour commodious for commerce and navigation.

Proclamation encouraging emigration to Jamaica

In the event, there was no great rush to take up this offer. The only significant number of settlers who went to Jamaica and the other islands in the 1650s were prisoners sentenced to transportation and orphans obliged to serve as indentured apprentices. Judged by this measure, the Protectorate's colonial settlement policy would appear to have been of little import. However, the essence of the argument of those historians who still regard it as significant is that, regardless of its immediate failure, it established a vital precedent. For the first time in English history central government had undertaken the responsibility of promoting organised overseas settlement, rather than leave it as a matter of individual or group enterprise. Thus the basis for imperial expansion had been laid.

Determinist historians - those who read history in terms of class struggle - often interpret Protectorate foreign policy as the pursuit of bourgeois (middle-class) goals. They suggest that the extension of British claims overseas illustrates the preponderance of commercial motives among the new middle class, who wished their government to grant them the opportunities for the furtherance of trade and commerce. In this regard, Cromwell is seen as representing, whether consciously or not, the new bourgeois thrust.

This line of reasoning does not go unchallenged. Steve Pincus, for example, doubts whether Cromwell thought in terms of establishing an empire in the later sense of the word. Pincus regards the Western Design as having been concerned not so much with the establishment of overseas territories, as with breaking the power of Spain in Europe by denying her resources from her American colonies. Other historians have also pointed out how difficult it is to reconcile the view of Cromwell as an agent of the bourgeoisie with those aspects of his policy where he followed religious aims in apparent disregard of their commercial or economic consequence. The problems he experienced throughout his Protectorship with the merchants hardly supports the notion that he was their representative.

e) Relations with France

Cromwell, while acknowledging that France was a Catholic power, was impressed by the willingness of the Bourbon monarchy to tolerate the Huguenots (French Protestants). It had been pointed out to him that this toleration was more honoured in the breach than in the observance, but his personal relations with Cardinal Mazarin, the French Chief Minister between 1654 and 1661, had convinced him that France would make a better ally than an enemy. Accordingly, given the limited success of the Spanish war, he was prepared to consider an agreement with France. The French were eager. They had been hoping for some time to win the new English government to their side in their long-running war with Spain.

The path to better Anglo-French relations was eased by French co-operation over a notorious incident in 1655. In May the Protectorate government learned of the massacre of hundreds of Protestants in the Alpine Vaudois valley, carried out by the troops of the Duke of Savoy. Cromwell, acting as the defender of the persecuted Protestants of Europe, protested angrily to the duke:

1 Oliver, Protector, to the most serene Prince Emmanuel, Duke of Savoy, Prince of Piedmont, greeting: We understand that such of your Royal Highness's subjects as professed the reformed religion are commanded to depart their native habitations and that when
5 they applied to your Royal Highness for a revocation of the edict, a part of your army fell upon them most cruelly, slew several, put others in chains and compelled the rest to fly into desert places and to mountains covered with snow, where some hundreds of families are reduced to such distress that tis greatly to be feared they will in
10 a short time perish through cold and hunger. These things when they were related to us, we could not choose but be touched with extreme grief and compassion for the sufferings and calamities of this afflicted people and we most earnestly beseech your Royal Highness that you would command their losses to be repaired and
15 that an end be put to their oppressions.

Since Savoy was an ally of France, Cromwell was also able to turn to the French to support his appeal. They responded sympathetically. French pressure was applied to Savoy with the result that the persecution of the Protestants in the area was halted. This positive response on the part of France helped further to prepare the way for a formal agreement, which was duly reached in October 1655 in the shape of a defensive alliance. One considerable gain for Cromwell was that the French agreed that they would no longer give shelter to the Stuarts.

England, a Protestant power, was now in alliance with France, a Catholic power, against Spain, another Catholic power. Whatever this betokened it obviously would not be logical to think of it as a religious struggle. National prestige and economic rivalry seem to have been more important factors. In March 1657 the original Anglo-French alliance was transformed into a military agreement. Under its terms contingents of Protectorate troops joined with the French to assist in an attack upon Spanish Flanders. Decisive victories came with the capture of Mardyke in October 1657 and at the Battle of the Dunes in the following June. One result of this latter victory was that England acquired the port of Dunkirk. The war with Spain outlived Oliver Cromwell and was not finally ended until May 1659 when France and Spain made peace in the Treaty of the Pyrenees.

f) The Baltic Question

Cromwell's dealings with the Baltic powers further illustrate the difficulty in the 1650s of trying to base foreign policy on purely religious concerns. Cromwell had marked personal respect for Charles X, the Swedish king, and hoped that their two countries might form some kind of Protestant union. An additional advantage of this would be to give England an *entrée* directly into Baltic diplomacy. The growing importance, commercially, of the Baltic powers with their large navies made it imperative that a major trading nation like Britain should have a direct say in such affairs. Neither the Protector nor the Swedish king was happy with the continued dominance in that region of the Dutch, who had established a disproportionate commercial advantage. In 1654 Sweden and England entered into a treaty intended to weaken the Dutch grip upon trade and to counterbalance an existing treaty between Holland and Denmark. Since all four of these countries were Protestant, religious considerations can hardly be said to have been of any relevance in their relations. There was certainly no sign among the Scandinavian and Baltic nations that they were prepared to suspend their economic rivalry for the sake of a Protestant league against the likes of Spain or France.

Although Charles X frequently expressed commitment to the Protestant cause, this appears to have been done largely to retain the Protectorate's favour in his difficult relations with his Baltic rivals. He was largely successful in this. In 1655 and again in 1657, when Sweden was in danger of being opposed by a combination of other Baltic states, Cromwell was prepared, against the wishes of the pro-Dutch lobby in England, to provide Charles X with both ships and money. However, in the last year of his life, it appeared that Cromwell had begun to doubt the value of the Anglo-Swedish connection and to fear that Sweden was becoming too powerful in the Baltic. Richard Cromwell adopted this same attitude during his brief period as Protector. During a further Baltic crisis in 1658-9 he supported Denmark and Holland in their resistance to Sweden's control of the Sound, a vital waterway which gave access to the Baltic. Richard declared that England would not tolerate such a threat to the free passage of her merchant ships. In the event, Sweden backed off, but Richard's response was taken by many as clear proof that his father's pro-Swedish policy had been based on a misreading of the situation.

4 The Debate on Cromwellian Foreign Policy

In describing foreign policy during the Interregnum historians have tended to fall into one of two camps: those who see it as basically a continuation of the traditional anti-Catholic policy dating from the time of Elizabeth I, and those who regard it as a new progressive policy in which commercial considerations predominated. The weight of modern opinion is that Cromwell's policies were essentially dated, that in a world that had rapidly changed into one of commercial competition, he still clung to an Elizabethan idea of a post-Reformation religious alignment. The obvious example is his attitude to Spain. Spain was declining as a world power and her place was being taken by France, yet Cromwell persisted in giving priority to what he perceived as the Spanish threat. This accounts for the quarrel that he then had with the merchant representatives in government and parliament. They pointed out that to persevere with policies based upon dubious interpretations of religious interests was to endanger England's far more important economic concerns.

During the 1650s relations between the European states were never simply a matter of religious affiliation. Catholic France remained at war with Catholic Spain, Protestant England fought against Protestant Holland, and Protestant Sweden went to war first with Catholic Poland and then with Protestant Denmark. Such complexity doomed any attempt to follow a purely confessional approach in foreign affairs. There are strong grounds for suggesting that by the end of the Thirty Years War secular considerations had began to take precedence over religion in shaping national attitudes. That is why Cromwell's sincere attempts to forge a Protestant alliance appear so anachronistic.

A question to which a great deal of attention is now being paid is how much authority Cromwell exercised personally over the shaping of foreign policy. He was, of course, the outstanding figure of his time and there has been an understandable tendency to think of him as the initiator of the policies of the Protectorate. Certain historians, notably Barry Coward, are anxious to point out that the evidence, while not entirely clear, suggests that he was not always a free agent. The pressures he imposed upon others were probably balanced by those he felt himself to be under.

It may be that modern analysts try too hard to determine the principles underlying Cromwell's foreign policy. It is doubtful whether he ever had the luxury of conducting his policy according to a predetermined plan. It is much more likely that he framed his policy on a day-to-day basis, conscious that circumstances required immediate responses. In 1656 the Venetian ambassador in London recorded the strain borne by Cromwell and his Council: 'They are so fully occupied they do not know which way to turn, and the protector has not a moment to call his own'. For later historians to distinguish between religious, commercial and national motivation in his policy, is somewhat artificial. Cromwell was trying in a very brief period of time to adapt to a changing diplomatic and military situation in Europe, in which the outstanding feature was the complexity and interaction of the motives that applied.

It should be stressed that Cromwell had little experience of foreign policy before he became Protector. Commenting on Cromwell's approach to foreign affairs, Slingsby Bethel remarked dryly that the Protector 'was not guilty of too much knowledge of them'. Cromwell's approach to other countries, therefore, was very much that of the prejudiced Englishman, who shared the prevailing distrust of Catholicism and fear of Papal encroachment on English interests. This necessarily coloured his attitude to Catholic states, but as Protector and therefore a European statesman, he was obliged to temper his prejudice with the realities of the European diplomatic situation. He never entirely lost his conviction that Spain was uniquely evil, but circumstances forced him to acknowledge that other nations represented a comparable threat, whether religious or commercial, to English concerns.

5 How Successful was Protectorate Foreign Policy?

Undeniably, Cromwell increased England's reputation among foreign nations, so much so that throughout the period of the Protectorate the English royalists had no realistic chance of gaining allies in Europe who were willing to risk supporting an attempted Stuart restoration. English diplomats, who had been often treated with disdain in Europe in the early years of the Commonwealth, found themselves respected and courted in the days of the Protectorate. Andrew Marvell, the poet, wrote that Cromwell 'once more joined us to the continent', while Samuel Pepys, the diarist, declared that 'he made all the neighbour princes fear him'. The royalist historian, Clarendon, made a remarkable summary of Cromwell's achievements:

1 To reduce three nations, which perfectly hated him to an entire obedience, to all his dictates; to awe and govern those nations by an army that was indevoted to him, and wished his ruin, was an instance of a very prodigious address. But his greatness at home
5 was but a shadow of the glory he had abroad. It was hard to discover which feared him the most, France, Spain, or the Low Countries.

Yet, whatever the success of Cromwell's foreign policy in terms of increased national prestige, it has to be emphasised that this was bought at a heavy domestic price. Foreign policy proved extremely costly; maintaining effective naval squadrons was a drain on already limited resources and his attempts to raise grants for their upkeep increased the tension between him and his parliaments.

In one area Cromwell clearly failed. His dreams of a Protestant federation against Spain and anti-Christ came to nothing, largely because European politics had changed. As the later stages of the Thirty Years war had shown religion was no longer the major determinant of international relations. Cromwell's slowness to appreciate this led him to persevere with policies that in many respects were out of date.

Cromwell's Western Design was only a partial success, but it paved the way for a French treaty. Although in one obvious sense alliance with a Catholic power compromised his original concept of a Protestant crusade, it enabled him to gain greater protection for the Huguenots and the Vaudois Protestants. The alliance also led in time to England's regaining Dunkirk, a toe-hold in Europe at the expense of Spain. It is also arguable that, whether intended or not, the Western Design marked the beginning of a colonial policy that in time would lead to the creation of the British empire.

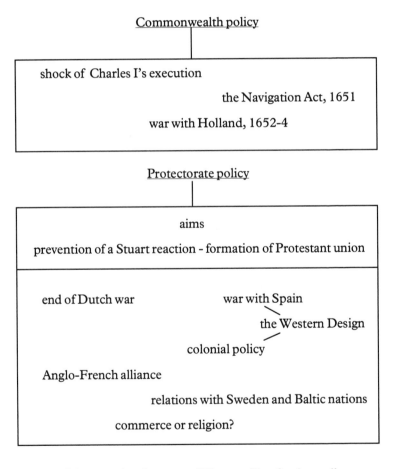

Commonwealth policy

shock of Charles I's execution

the Navigation Act, 1651

war with Holland, 1652-4

Protectorate policy

aims

prevention of a Stuart reaction - formation of Protestant union

end of Dutch war   war with Spain

the Western Design

colonial policy

Anglo-French alliance

relations with Sweden and Baltic nations

commerce or religion?

the debate on the character of Cromwellian foreign policy

Summary - Foreign Policy During the Interregnum

Making notes on 'Foreign Policy During the Interregnum'

Foreign policy can be tricky to study unless you have a working knowledge of the main features of the international scene. That is why it is worth making sure you have grasped the principal ideas in the Background section. Two themes dominate the period; England's wars, first with Holland and then with Spain. Use sections 1 and 2 to acquaint yourself with the origin and outcome of these wars. A helpful framework for your notes might be as follows:

Q. Why war with Holland?

A. Impact of Charles I's execution - commercial rivalry -Dutch gains from Thirty Years War - failure of Rump's mission -Navigation Act. Under each of the sub-sections of your response, you might care to note further points of detail, drawn from the relevant part of the chapter. For example, under the sub-heading, 'commercial rivalry' appropriate points would be Anglo-Dutch trade competition in Europe and the East Indies and the long-running dispute over fishing grounds. A similar form of breakdown-analysis can be applied to the Spanish war.

Since Cromwell is so significant a figure, it is important to gain an understanding of the debate that still surrounds his foreign policy. This is best done by following the treatment in sections 4 and 5, which offers an analysis of his motivation in foreign policy and an assessment of his achievement in this field.

Answering essay questions on 'Foreign Policy During the Interregnum'

Conrad Russell, one of the major modern authorities of the period, has suggested that the reason why Protectorate foreign policy receives such a large amount of attention from historians is because it makes an excellent subject for examination questions! His jest has a serious and consoling aspect, for there is indeed a self-contained character about the subject that should make it attractive to the student. Exam questions most frequently ask about the motivation behind Protectorate policy. Consider these typical examples:

1   Was the foreign policy of the Commonwealth and Protectorate based upon consistent principles?
2   How far did the Dutch war of 1652-4 serve British interests?
3   Was the Western Design 'grander in concept than in achievement'?
4   To what extent was Oliver Cromwell's foreign policy determined by religious considerations?
5   Consider the view that 'there was never a single Protectorate foreign policy, only a number of policies'.
6   'Aggressive imperialist ... protestant zealot': which is the more

appropriate description of Oliver Cromwell in his conduct of foreign policy?

7   Was Oliver Cromwell's foreign policy an anachronism?

Although the questions differ in form, the essential thrust is the same in each. What is being sought is an analysis of the underlying aims of Protectorate policy. The list divides neatly into two groups; the first set deal with the Protectorate broadly, the second with Oliver Cromwell directly. Your task is to judge the weighting to give to your material. This will vary from question to question. One of the persistent weaknesses in exam answers is their failure to be relevant to the particular question being tackled. Compare questions 3 and 5. Obviously there is considerable overlap of material, but test yourself by deciding which of the following points should go into each answer: Cromwell's bitterness against Spain, his hopes of a Protestant union, English emnity towards the Spanish empire, the unsuccessful attack upon Hispaniola and the taking of Jamaica, England's relations with France and Holland, merchant objections to the Western Design, the degree of Cromwell's personal involvement in the Design, encouragement of colonial emigration.

Source-based questions on 'Foreign Policy During the Interregnum'

1 The Spanish Question
Study Cromwell's assertions on page 78 and the illustration on page 80. Answer the following questions.
a) Explain Cromwell's reference to 'an empire of such vast and prodigious extent' (line 3, page 78). (5 marks)
b) Using your own knowledge and the evidence in the illustration, describe the main features of 'the black legend of Spain'. (6 marks)
c) In what ways do these two sources contribute to an understanding of the reasons for the undertaking by the Protectorate of the Western Design? (8 marks)

2 The aims of Protectorate Foreign Policy
Study Cromwell's letter on page 84 and the Proclamation on page 82, and then answer the following questions.
a) Using your own knowledge and the evidence in the Proclamation, explain the developments that led to Jamaica becoming an area of British immigration in the 1650s. (6 marks)
b) How would you explain the tone and style adopted by Cromwell in his letter to the Duke of Savoy? (7 marks)
c) In what ways does Cromwell's appeal to the Duke relate to the development of the Protectorate's relations with France? (6 marks)
d) How useful are the Proclamation and the appeal as evidence of the character of Protectorate foreign policy? (8 marks)

CHAPTER 6

The Path to Restoration, 1658-60

It is important not to read history in reverse and assume that there was a logical, if not inevitable, drift towards monarchy during the two years after Oliver Cromwell's death. The predominant feature was the uncertainty of the times. The contending groups were clearer about what they did not want than about what they did. Opportunism rather than clearly thought-out strategies became the order of the day. As in any situation where the political system is weak or confused, the power of the sword predominated. Much as the civilian and religious groups may have disliked the presence of the military, it was the army that held the key to any settlement. This had been true since the execution of Charles I in 1649. That truth was re-emphasised in the period following Oliver Cromwell's death. Protector Oliver may not have been overwhelmingly popular, but even his opponents could admire his military prowess. As long as he was at the helm disorder had been contained. But with his passing nothing was certain anymore.

The many twists and turns of this period make it a complex one. It is helpful, therefore, to break it down into its essential features. In outline these were as follows:

1 The Protectorate of Richard Cromwell, September 1658 - April 1659
   a) the Third Protectorate Parliament, January-April 1659
2 The Restored Commonwealth, May 1659 - February 1660
   a) the Recalled Rump, May-October 1659
   b) the Committee of Safety, October-December 1659
   c) The Recalled Rump, December 1659 - February 1660
3 The Restored Long Parliament, February - March 1660
4 The Convention Parliament, April - May 1660
5 The Restoration of Monarchy - May 1660

1 The Protectorate under Richard Cromwell, September 1658 - April 1659

In September 1658, under the terms of the *Humble Petition and Advice*, Richard Cromwell duly succeeded his father as Lord Protector and Commander-in-Chief. Great as Oliver Cromwell's difficulties had been, he had managed to preserve an uneasy balance between the demands of army, the religious radicals and the traditionalists. But he had been able to do this only through his personal authority and power. The permanence he had sought had eluded him. He had not created the new form of self-sustaining civilian government that he so much desired. The Protectorship that he bequeathed to his son was dependent on the willingness of the army to continue supporting it.

Richard Cromwell inherited a situation which contained four main political groupings: the army, the republicans (Commonwealthsmen), the Presbyterians, and the radical sectaries. To these could be added a fifth element, the royalists. Although they had been subdued during Oliver Cromwell's time, his death and the diffidence of the new Protector encouraged them to action again. What gave them cause for hope was that the Presbyterians who had been disturbed by the socially-disruptive notions among the sectaries had become more reactionary in their attitude. They had never been wholly reconciled to the republic; the religious settlement which they had hoped for had not materialised. They were quite prepared, therefore, to consider alliance with the royalists, not out of love for monarchy, but because the alternative to monarchy was social disorder and religious factionalism.

Another important political feature was the lack of unity among the army leaders. Fleetwood and a number of the senior officers saw it as being to their advantage to maintain the Protectorate, since, with an inexperienced Protector, they felt they would be able to control the situation. However, the tendency among the lower ranks was to side with the sectaries, who were unhappy with a Protector who seemed to have distinct Presbyterian sympathies. This group called for a return to the Commonwealth, which would mean a return to 1653 and a reinstating of the Rump Parliament.

How deep Richard's Presbyterianism went is difficult to judge, but his uneasy relationship with the army certainly led him to rely increasingly on civilian advisers of a conservative outlook. Richard's besetting weakness as Protector was that he was not a soldier. Hitherto, he had lived as a country squire, showing little aptitude for either military or political affairs. He now found himself thrust deeply into both. Unlike his father, he could not call on the natural loyalty of the army. This left him only one recourse, to turn towards the civilian elements in government.

The difficulty of Richard's relations with the military soon showed itself when they urged him to give up his position as Commander-in-Chief. At first he refused, which brought fierce criticism from the leading generals, Desborough and Fleetwood. Richard tried to counterbalance this by cultivating the more sympathetic officers. He had some success; Walley and Gough, who had ruled as Major-Generals in 1655, and George Monk, the Commander of the English army of occupation in Scotland, were some of the more notable officers who sided with Richard.

However, the bulk of the army was not to be won over. There was still deep resentment over the perennial problem of army arrears of pay; the collective sum owed to the troops was £900,000. This was an aspect of the overall financial difficulties of the Protectorate. It was falling increasingly into debt. At the beginning of 1659 this was calculated at £2,500,000. The Protectorate's expenditure continued to run ahead of its revenue. The situation was not eased by the general economic depression that England was experiencing. One particularly troublesome feature of this was the high price of food, which followed a series of poor harvests and a severe trade recession in the late-1650s. As had his father and Charles I before him, Richard was obliged to call parliament in order to raise money.

a) The Third Protectorate Parliament, January-April 1659

Given the conflicting opinions it represented, Parliament was unlikely to give Richard a comfortable time. Since there was no formal party system corresponding to the various political groups, it is not easy to give precise figures, but, in a House of 549 members, pro-Protectorate conservatives seem to have been in the majority. Unfortunately for Richard, the republican minority proved much more active and vociferous; it launched into a series of attacks on the legitimacy of the Protectorate. The republicans made a particular bid to rally support among the army. Fearing that such tactics would play into the hands of those who wanted to tighten the military's grip on affairs still further, the conservative presbyterian MPs attempted to undermine the army's power. They introduced a resolution that the Council of Officers should sit only with the permission of Parliament, and voted to take the command of the local militia out of the hands of the army and bring it under direct parliamentary control. Officers and ranks united in the face of this response and demanded that the Protector dissolve Parliament. Richard resisted, but when he learned that England was on the verge of an army insurrection, he eventually gave way and did as he was bid.

Little was now left of his authority. It was clear that he wanted to move towards a predominantly civil administration by reducing the influence of the standing army, but it was equally clear that the military would not allow this. With the dissolution of Parliament against Richard's wishes, power was effectively back in the hands of the Council of the Army, some of whom, including Fleetwood, were prepared to allow the Protectorate to continue, provided it left the army in charge. However, in order to make their power appear somewhat less stark, the Council recommended the recalling of the Rump, a move that was highly pleasing to the Commonwealthsmen who felt that their republican agitation was obviously having an effect.

The Rump re-assembled in May 1659. The end of the Protectorate was not long delayed. Richard Cromwell, having tried unavailingly to summon loyal troops from Ireland and Scotland, resigned and withdrew from public life. Three features explain his failure as Protector: his inability to fashion a civil government free of army control, the strength of the republican campaign against the Protectorate, and the financial bankruptcy into which his government sank. Richard Cromwell was not particularly incompetent, but effective government in the situation created by his father's death required a leader of extraordinary talent. Richard Cromwell was not extraordinary; he was a stolid, honest, squire, who lacked the political and governmental skills that the times demanded.

2 The Restored Commonwealth, May 1659-February 1660

a) The Rump Recalled, May-October 1659

The resurrected Rump soon showed itself to be the same in character and attitude as when it had been dispersed six years earlier. It declined to acknowledge its dependence on the army with whose leaders it was soon at odds. It tried to behave as if the events of the intervening six years had not taken place. It denounced the army's interference in political matters, and claimed legitimacy as the only authority representing constitutional continuity. The army's duty was thus to obey the parliament it had restored. The faint possibility of this happening disappeared when it became apparent to the army leaders that the Rump had no intention of giving priority to their requests for reform. In particular, they were angered by the Rump's failure to attend to the question of the troops' arrears of pay. The truth was that the two bodies regarded each other as little more than a regrettable necessity. The Rump knew that to preserve itself in troubled times an army was necessary to maintain the peace. For its part, the army appreciated that the Rump served to clothe what would otherwise be recognised as naked military rule.

The irony was that in the country at large the Rump was thought to be too radical. What encouraged this idea was that in a number of counties the restored Rump had made an attempt to curb the influence of the army by deliberately putting the local militia into the hands of the extreme sectaries, including Fifth Monarchists, Quakers and Baptists. This strange development excited fears of a takeover by the religious extremists. There were even rumours that the Levellers were re-organising. The outpouring of pamphlets in 1659 gave the superficial impression that the radical forces were much stronger than they were. It was this that frightened the conservatives into retreating further towards a restoration of the old constitution.

Something approaching national panic occurred. There was talk of church and state being under threat from radical forces. It was in this disturbed atmosphere that a series of scattered Presbyterian-royalist risings took place in the summer of 1659. These were less a genuine attempt to restore the Stuart monarchy than an outburst of irritation at what the Rump was allowing to happen. The government acted quickly. Forewarned of the conspiracies, they were able to break them with a series of pre-emptive military strikes.

The one serious challenge was in Cheshire, where, in August 1659,

Sir George Booth held large parts of the county in defiance of the Rump. Booth did not actually call for a return of Charles II, but for a 'free parliament'. This amounted to much the same thing, since it was believed that a freely-elected parliament would be the prelude to a royal restoration. But the fact that he did not openly advocate Charles II's return shows how relatively weak royalism was at this point. It was the disgruntled Presbyterians rather than the royalist supporters of Charles who were making the challenge, thus suggesting that it was more an expression of anti-Rump sentiment than a genuinely pro-Stuart movement. Booth held on for a number of weeks, but his expectation that Spanish troops would arrive to assist him proved wildly unrealistic and he eventually surrendered.

There now seemed to be an opportunity for the radicals to establish a hold on England. The Presbyterians and their conservative allies had been broken, and the army had again shown itself able to overcome any royalist challenge. However, the radicals were too ill-defined a group to constitute a single source of opinion, let alone power. The divisions between the religious sectaries, who still hankered after the rule of the saints, and the republicans, who wanted a single-chamber secular parliament, prevented a unified radical approach. There was something very unreal, therefore, about the long debates over possible constitutional change that occupied so much of the Rump's time in the summer and autumn of 1659. The truth was that no settlement could satisfy the wide range of the radicals' political and religious opinions. Still more important, no settlement stood a chance of being adopted unless it first met the approval of the army.

The crushing of Booth's rising had been directed by John Lambert. His military success put him back in the political limelight. He became the hero of the rank and file in the army's growing dispute with the Rump. Lambert gave his support to an army petition which demanded that the Rump's authority be reduced by the creation of a Senate (upper house) and that the army leaders be all promoted to the rank of general and confirmed in their command. The petition also insisted that the army be granted authority to purge all those local corporations that had not actively opposed the recent royalist risings. The reaction of the Rump was to see this as a direct attempt on the part of the army to usurp political authority. Arthur Haselrig moved that Lambert and his fellow petitioners be removed and imprisoned. The animosity between Lambert and Haselrig who were respectively the leading military and civilian republicans was an indication of how far republicanism was from being a cohesive movement. Haselrig hoped that there were still enough troops faithful to parliament to prevent an army coup. But he had miscalculated. Retaliation came quickly. In October, regiments loyal to Lambert occupied London and forcibly dissolved the Rump.

b) The Committee of Safety, October-December 1659

There was now nothing to hide the reality of military rule. The army had previously brought down the Protectorate; it had now broken the remaining link with the old constitution. England found herself again without a legitimate government. Authority lay with the Council of the Army. In an attempt to give its power the semblance of constitutional propriety, the Council appointed a 'Committee of Safety', an interim government, composed of the officers and a few token civilians, until a more permanent body could be established.

The Army Council's dispersal of the Rump had been swift and effective, but it had not won the unanimous support of the army. This was soon evident in the reaction of General George Monk, the Commander in Scotland and someone destined to become the critical figure in the events leading to the Restoration. Monk protested at the dissolution of the Rump. He negotiated with the members of the expelled House, who offered him the post of Commander-in-Chief and invited him to bring his army south to London. Monk prepared to do so and issued a justification for his action; he claimed to have received:

a call from God and his people to march into England, to assist and maintain the liberty and being of parliaments, our ancient constitution, and therein the freedom and rights of the people of these three nations from arbitrary and tyrannical usurpations.

The Army Council first tried to dissuade Monk from continuing his march. When this failed they despatched Lambert north to intercept him. But Lambert's forces were no match for Monk's in either morale or discipline. They disintegrated with scarcely a fight.

Monk's protest at the Rump's dissolution and his easy victory over Lambert gave a considerable lift to the forces opposed to army rule. The internal divisions within the army encouraged serious challenges. Widespread disturbances occurred between October and December, notably in Bristol and London. Portsmouth, an important garrison town, declared against the government, as did the navy. It was as if all those unhappy with the prevailing system were now prepared to risk openly challenging it. The Committee of Safety was taken aback by the sheer scale of the pent-up anger that expressed itself. The seriousness of the disorders in London may be gauged from the following description by the French ambassador of the time.

1 About the end of last week it was discovered that, at the instigation of some Presbyterian ministers, royalists and old parliamentarians, some apprentices of this town proposed to get up a requisition tending to the convocation of a free parliament, or to the recall of
5 the last, and to the maintenance of the churches. The Committee

of Safety directed the Mayor of London to publish a prohibition to
proceed further in the matter on pain of indictment for treason. He
did not refuse to obey; nevertheless under the pretext of
indisposition and fear of the people, the officers whose duty it is to
10 perform this act refused to do it, and the Mayor being again called
upon asked time to confer with his Common Council. But,
without waiting until its deliberations were over, a company of
cavalry proceeded to the front of the Exchange and attempted to
make the proclamation. The apprentices did not fail to gather
15 around and to interrupt it by yells, even to maltreat the trumpeters
and mingle among the horsemen, who not finding themselves
strong enough to withstand the populace, retired in disorder and
were pursued as far as St.Paul's Church where there is a garrison.
Immediately, all the cavalry and infantry which had been posted in
20 different parts of the town took arms, and marched through the
streets in order of battle, and one regiment went to take possession
of the neighbourhood of the Exchange. The apprentices having
continued still to irritate them with words, and even with stones,
the soldiers fired upon the people, only two of whom were killed.
25 The shops were shut.

Protest petitions poured in to the Committee of Safety and to the City of
London. Monk was also inundated with petitions as he made his way
south. The three commonest themes in all of these were the grim
economic circumstances of the day, the tyranny of army rule, and the
need for the restoration of ancient liberties through a free parliament or
monarchy.

1 It hath pleased the good and only wise God for our and the
Nations' crying sins to manifest his displeasure for many years
together against these once flourishing, now sadly divided,
distracted and almost ruined Nations: and yet blessed be God, this
5 Honourable City hitherto hath been no Proportionable sharer in
the calamities which our Brethren in other parts of these now
miserable nations have suffered, which are now aggravated by our
divisions, and such a general decay of trading, as doth exceed the
worst of former times. (from a Petition of the London apprentices)

10 Since the death of the King, we have been governed by tumult;
bandied from one faction to the other; this party up today, that
tomorrow - but still the nation under, and a prey to, the strongest.
So long as this violence continues over us, no other government
can settle the nation than that which pleases the universality of it.
15 You speak of the necessity of a republic. We say it is not necessary,
nor even effectual, but if it were both, a free parliament ought to
introduce it. The Consent of the people must settle the nation, the

public debt must be secured out of the public stock, and interests of opinion and property must be secured by a free parliament.
20 (from a Petition of the Gentlemen of Devon)

We are filled with howlings; our trades are generally lost, and there is none to give us work; our wool, and leather, and corn, and butter, and cheese, are daily transported and whilst we are lessened in our manufactures, and vocations and industries, we are raised in
25 rents, and food, and taxes, and all things belonging to our livelihood; the mysteries of our crafts, and the materials of our manufactures, do find such acceptable receipt in foreign parts, as unconscionable men have brought the ruins of their own country into a trade; and those laws, which for the chief benefit of the
30 people, and the very life of trade, are made, are so boldly affronted (from 'Awake O England')

Fleetwood and the army officers bowed before this storm of opposition and rather than face a renewal of civil war allowed the Rump to re-assemble in December 1659. This achieved Monk's immediate objective, but he continued his march south. His troops crossed the Scottish-English border on New Year's day 1660 and reached London in February.

c) The Recalled Rump, December 1659-February 1660

What the second recalling of the Rump showed was the deep unpopularity of the army's rule up to that point. The paradox was that army authority could be removed only by the exercise of further military power. None of the civil institutions was capable in itself of resisting the army. The re-installing of the Rump in December could not have been achieved without the intervention of Monk. It was his action that had forced the Committee of Safety to dissolve itself and permit the Rump's reassembly.

The climb-down of the army leaders caused a major political shift; the conservative forces began to recover. Desborough, Lambert and Fleetwood were dismissed by the Rump and replaced, and Monk was invited to become Commander-in-Chief. The Rump now appeared to be in a strong position. It had removed the army leaders, re-established itself as a parliament and government and had the backing of Monk, the most powerful general in the land. But it then proceeded to throw away its advantage by a series of fatal mistakes. Instead of attending to the nation's problems and grievances, it seemed more concerned with settling old scores. It undertook what amounted to a purge of the army. Half the serving officers were removed. Although it might be argued that there was a certain justice in this, the vindictive spirit in which it was done and the corruption and nepotism that accompanied the appointment of new officers and officials did not speak well for the integrity of the Rump. Certainly, there was a broad public distaste for their proceedings, illustrated clearly in a widespread refusal by traders and merchants to pay parliamentary taxes.

The Rump also showed its ineptitude in the way it treated Monk after his arrival in London in February. Rather than honouring him as its saviour, which he undoubtedly was, it sought to restrict his influence politically by instructing him to busy himself with the policing of London, which was still in an excited and volatile mood. However, Monk refused to be overawed; he did use his troops to bring order to the City, but he was not to be deterred from involvement in the politics that had brought him south in the first place. He insisted that the Rump confirm the promise given to him that it would not sit beyond May 1660. More significantly still, he outmanoeuvred those MPs who claimed that the Rump was now the sovereign power by re-admitting to the House the 'secluded' members - those who had been debarred at the time of Pride's Purge in 1648.

3 The Restored Long Parliament, February-March 1660

Monk's insistence that the secluded MPs be permitted to retake their seats had striking results. The return of a substantial number of members of the pre-1649 Long Parliament altered the political balance. Although their ranks had been depleted by death over the intervening ten years, they were still a large enough group to tilt the scales against Haselrig's republican faction. Since they had not been implicated in the trial of Charles I or the creation of the Commonwealth, they represented a direct constitutional link with 1642. The claim of the Rump and of the Army Council to direct events had rested ultimately on the legitimacy of Pride's Purge and the execution of the King. Allowing the secluded members to return amounted to a denial of that legitimacy and made a restoration of the Stuart monarchy much more likely. The first steps towards this were soon evident in parliament's turning of the tables by excluding from its ranks members known to be of strong republican sympathies. Lambert was a prominent victim of this purge.

At the time of the recall of the Long Parliament Monk was careful not to declare openly that he was working for an eventual royal restoration. He wanted to avoid polarising the issue too early. He presented himself very much as the moderate, who, while being resolute against extremists, understood and was prepared to tolerate all forms of responsible opinion. He persuaded parliament to keep its promise to make him Commander-in-Chief, to appoint a new Council of State, and then to vote for its own dissolution, preparatory to a new parliament being elected. Another push towards a royal restoration was given by the Long Parliament's reappointment of Edward Montague, a former Cromwellian general but now a royalist sympathiser, as Commander of the Fleet. This meant that the two leading military commanders, on land and at sea, now favoured Charles's return.

The tide was running strongly towards a royal restoration. Whether this had been Monk's intention all along remains uncertain, but it is significant that as early as the previous July he had entered into a very cordial correspondence with the exiled Charles II. Charles's trust in Monk was clearly expressed in a letter he wrote early in their negotiations.

> 1 I am confident that George Monk can have no malice in his heart against me; nor hath he done anything against me which I cannot easily pardon, and it is in his power to do me so great service, that I cannot easily reward, but I will do all I can; and I do authorize you
> 5 to treat with him; and not only to assure him of my kindness, but that I will very liberally reward him with such an estate in land, and such a title of honour as himself shall desire, if he will declare for me, and adhere to my interest.

4 The Convention Parliament, April-May 1660

While the elections for the new parliament were being held, Lambert made one last bid to save the republican cause. He attempted to halt the movement towards a royal restoration by a show of force. A number of regiments supported him, but the bulk of the army declined to challenge Monk. Fleetwood and Desborough made no move; neither did Haselrig, the leading civilian republican. In an ironically appropriate final engagement at Edgehill, the site in 1642 of the first of the civil war battles, Lambert's army was defeated and he was captured.

Monk had overcome the republicans militarily. The election results now showed that his mixture of tact and shrewdness had undermined them politically. Although the writs for the election had specified that no known royalists were entitled to stand, this was widely ignored; over 60 members with strong royalist leanings took seats in the new House. In contrast, republicans and supporters of the Commonwealth did badly. This was not unexpected. What it proved was that the holding of genuinely free elections encouraged the return of members of royalist sympathies.

The new parliament, known as the Convention Parliament, gathered on 25 April. The House of Lords was re-convened and the joint Houses then considered the terms for restoration which Charles had previously offered in his Declaration of Breda issued on 4 April.

5 The Restoration of Monarchy, May 1660

In a sense, all Charles II needed to do after Monk's dramatic entry into

English politics six months earlier was to wait and do nothing. He had shown himself adept at this. His inaction proved decisive for it carried the impression that he was not seeking to impose himself upon the nation but was awaiting their invitation. His Declaration of Breda showed the same political acumen.

The Declaration, said to have been drafted by Clarendon, Charles's chief adviser in exile, was a skilful act of conciliation that revealed an astute perception of the outstanding grievances of the time and how they could be resolved. Charles promised a general pardon, religious toleration, and accepted the right of parliament to decide the disputed questions of property entitlements and the army's arrears of pay. The key passages read:

1 We do grant a free and general pardon to all our subjects ... Let all our subjects, how faulty soever, rely upon the word of a king, solemnly given by this present declaration, that no crime whatsoever, committed against us or our royal father before the
5 publication of this, shall ever rise in judgment, or be brought in question, against any of them, to the least endamagement of them.

... And because the passion and uncharitableness of the times have produced several opinions in religion, by which men are engaged in parties and animosities against each other ... we do declare a liberty
10 to tender consciences ...

And because, in the continued distractions of so many years, and so many and great revolutions, many grants and purchases of estates have been made to and by many officers, soldiers and others, who are now possessed of the same, and who may be liable
15 to actions at law upon several titles, we are likewise willing that all such differences, and all things relating to such grants, sales and purchases, shall be determined in parliament, which can best provide for the just satisfaction of all men who are concerned ...

And we do further declare, that we will be ready to consent to any
20 Act or Acts of Parliament to the purposes aforesaid, and for the full satisfaction of all arrears due to the officers and soldiers of the army under the command of General Monk

Both Houses voted to accept the Declaration as the constitutional basis for the restoration of the monarchy. On 8 May 1660 England was formally declared to be no longer a republic; government again resided in King, Lords and Commons. On 14 May a parliamentary deputation visited Charles to invite him to retake his throne. On 29 May King Charles II made a ceremonial entry into London.

6 Reasons for the Failure of the Republic

Within two years of Oliver Cromwell's death on 3 September 1658 the
Stuart monarchy had been restored in the person of Charles II. In one
obvious sense, this was a triumph of the royalist cause, but it would be
wrong to assume that it was simply royalist strength that brought it
about. Indeed, only ten months before Charles's return as King in May
1660, the royalist rising led by George Booth had been so poorly
supported and so easily crushed that it was said that Charles had
despaired of ever regaining his throne. The reasons for the Restoration
are, therefore, to be found less in royalist pressure than in the failure of
the republic to resolve the difficulties and contradictions that had
dogged it since its inception in 1649 and which became particularly
pronounced after Oliver Cromwell's death. In Gerald Aylmer's words:

1 Given the divisions and weaknesses among the Cromwellians and
  republicans, a Stuart restoration was probably unavoidable from
  September 1658 ... On the other hand, the precise time and
  manner of Charles II's return was by no means inevitable until
5 much nearer to the event, arguably not before February-March
  1660.

a) The Political Weakness of the Republic

There is a strong case for saying that part of Oliver Cromwell's problem
as Protector had been that he was not prepared to use force consistently
enough to impose a settlement to his liking. He persisted with his belief
that godly rule might be achieved by relying on the goodwill of honest
men. It is also arguable that after 1658 although the army frequently
interfered in affairs they never did so with sufficient clarity of purpose to
effect a lasting settlement. The army remained the final arbiter since no
solution would work that was not acceptable to them, but this was a
negative power; it did not guarantee that a solution could be found.
They could destroy, but they could not create. Moreover, there was
decreasing unity within the army. Again, this had been so even under
Oliver Cromwell, but his authority had been sufficient to maintain
obedience. Without him the conflicting attitudes among the officers
became much more evident.

The monarchy was restored because the republic had discredited
itself. The Protectorate created in 1653 had attempted to establish a
workable system of government based on a written constitution. With
the abandonment of the Protectorate in 1659, there was a power
vacuum, which the successive regimes were unable to fill. Lacking
constitutional credibility and sustained only by the authority of an
increasingly divided army, the republic had no claim on the nation's

loyalty. In the end the forces of conservatism proved stronger than those of radicalism.

b) The Unpopularity of Army Rule

What the period 1658-60 showed was that military rule was unwelcome to the majority of those in positions of social and political influence. For one thing it was hugely expensive. The cost of maintaining the army and navy meant the retention of heavy taxation, one of the grievances that had formerly done so much to poison the relations between king and parliament. No political settlement that threatened to maintain high taxes as part of its programme was likely to be acceptable to the established classes. London is a striking illustration of this. Ever since 1640 the capital had been one of the most dependable sources of parliamentary strength; throughout the 1650s it had backed the various governments of the Commonwealth and Protectorate. However, in 1659 large numbers of Londoners had become so embittered by the costs associated with military rule that they were willing to contemplate a return to monarchy. It was no mere coincidence that the first serious civilian challenge to the army came with the protest of the London apprentices against the Committee of Safety, and the organised tax boycott by the London merchants, in the autumn of 1659.

c) The Contribution of Monk

George Monk's particular skill was in being able to play the role of a moderate throughout the period leading up to the Restoration. This made him acceptable to that growing body of opinion that after nearly 20 years of unresolved turmoil wanted peace and social stability. He could have made a bid for personal power but chose not to; he seems to have genuinely wanted a civilian government. This is very reminiscent of Oliver Cromwell; like Cromwell his ability to influence events rested on his command of a reliable army. We again have the paradox of an army leader using his military authority to impose a civilian settlement. It could not have been achieved any other way. Without Monk, the royalists would not have been able to recover in the way that they did.

d) Divisions within the Army

A dominant characteristic of the the army in the period after Oliver Cromwell's death was its disunity. There was rivalry and jealousy among the leaders and unrest among the troops. The outstanding example of this was the disintegration of Lambert's forces when sent by the Committee of Safety to prevent Monk's march southwards. Their condition typified that of many of the regiments - unpaid, badly provisioned and reluctant to obey the orders of squabbling commanders. The chief complaint of the lower ranks was that the generals had yet to satisfy them in regard to the two demands that the troops had been making since the the civil wars began - full settlement of arrears of pay and indemnity against prosecution for past actions. It was ironic that in the end it was the return of Charles II that resolved these grievances. His promise of pay and indemnity, guarantees which the generals had not been able to deliver to their men in nearly 20 years of fighting, made monarchy appealing even to the rank and file.

e) The Attraction of Monarchy

Few people are wedded to constitutional forms on grounds of pure principle. Self-interest largely determines whether or not a particular system is acceptable. A republic that appeared to increase rather than lessen the financial burdens on the nation and to have no answer to the great social, political and religious questions of the day was finally judged not to be worth preserving.

In contrast, by 1660 a restored monarchy offered the hope of a return to political and religious stability, the end of the army's intrusion into civil affairs, and the re-establishment of the authority of the traditional ruling classes in central and local government. These were sufficiently powerful incentives to convince all but the most extreme religious or political radicals that the republic has outlived its usefulness.

'The old order was the natural order.' This telling sentence expresses the basic reason why the restoration occurred. All the other experiments had failed. None had been able to achieve stability or gain acceptance. All had been imposed and all had depended on the power of the army to maintain them.

Making notes on 'The Path to Restoration, 1658-60'

This theme requires two distinct aspects to be studied: the narrative of events, and the possible explanations for them. The first section of your notes, therefore, should provide you with the main signposts in the story. The titles of the sub-sections in this chapter are worth adopting as your own main headings. The second section should contain the key points of analysis; it would be very helpful if you were to compile two lists: of a) republican weaknesses, and of b) royalist strengths. In examination terms, the obvious central question is why the monarchy was restored less than two years after Oliver Cromwell's death. Your notes should all relate to this issue. The following list suggests how you might break this down into a manageable form. You will see that there are a number of questions under each heading. Attempt to answer these in notes. You will find this a highly effective way of testing whether you have understood the material in the chapter.

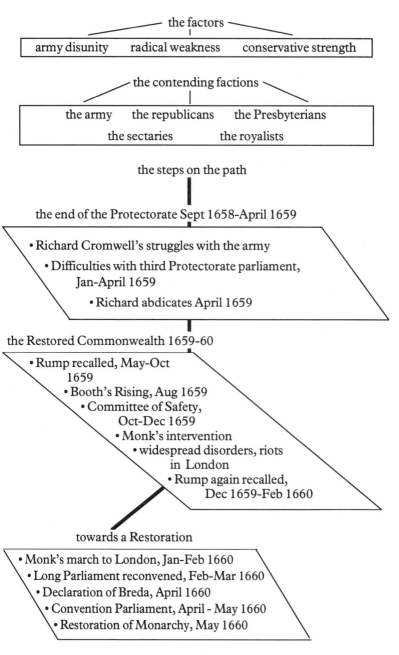

the factors

| army disunity | radical weakness | conservative strength |

the contending factions

| the army | the republicans | the Presbyterians |
| the sectaries | | the royalists |

the steps on the path

the end of the Protectorate Sept 1658-April 1659

- Richard Cromwell's struggles with the army
- Difficulties with third Protectorate parliament, Jan-April 1659
- Richard abdicates April 1659

the Restored Commonwealth 1659-60

- Rump recalled, May-Oct 1659
- Booth's Rising, Aug 1659
- Committee of Safety, Oct-Dec 1659
- Monk's intervention
- widespread disorders, riots in London
- Rump again recalled, Dec 1659-Feb 1660

towards a Restoration

- Monk's march to London, Jan-Feb 1660
- Long Parliament reconvened, Feb-Mar 1660
- Declaration of Breda, April 1660
- Convention Parliament, April - May 1660
- Restoration of Monarchy, May 1660

Summary - The Path to Restoration, 1658-60

1   The End of the Protectorate -the problems inherited by Richard
    Cromwell - Why was he not able to overcome them?
2   The Restored Commonwealth
    a) the Recalled Rump - What were the Rump's relations with the
    army?
    b) national unrest - What was the significance of Booth's Rising? -
    Why did the radicals fail to seize their opportunity?
3   The Committee of Safety - the dissolution of the Rump - Monk's
    reaction - the Recalled Rump - Why did the army lose control of the
    situation in December 1659?
4   The Restored Long Parliament - the role of Monk - the significance
    of the return of the 'Secluded members' - Why were the republicans
    defeated?
5   The Restoration of Monarchy - Charles II's tactics - the Convention
    Parliament - the return of the Lords - the Declaration Of Breda -
    Was the Restoration inevitable after February 1660?

Answering essay questions on *'The Path to Restoration, 1658-60'*

Although examination questions on this period may vary in emphasis
they all revolve around the central issue of why the republic collapsed in
the period 1658-60. Consider the following list:

1   'The problems bequeathed by Oliver Cromwell meant that
    Richard's Protectorate was doomed from the start.' Assess the
    accuracy of this statement.
2   Royalist strength or republican weakness: which was the more
    important factor in the events leading to the Restoration?
3   Examine the role played by the army in the period between the
    death of Oliver Cromwell and the restoration of Charles II.
4   How true is it to say that without Monk there would have been
    no restoration?
5   Why was it that the royalist cause failed in August 1659 but
    triumphed in May 1660?
6   How accurate is it to describe the period from September 1658
    to May 1660 as one of 'chaos'?
7   Why did republicanism have so few defenders in England by
    May 1660?
8   Examine the claim that 'It was the 20 months after his death that
    really showed how powerful Oliver Cromwell had been as
    Protector'.

The notes you have already compiled should allow you to approach all
these, confident that you have the necessary material to hand. What you
need to do is to judge the different weighting and emphasis that the
questions require. For example, questions 2, 5 and 7 are concerned with
assessing the respective strengths and weaknesses of the royalists and

republicans. Questions 3, 6 and 8 call for an overview of the whole period covered by the chapter, which means that you would have to be selective in your material in order not to become lost in detail. Questions 3 and 4 have obvious overlap; however, 3 is concerned with the full 20 months after September 1658, while 4 is directed particularly at the events from December 1659 onwards. Oliver Cromwell is specifically mentioned in 1 and 8, but ask yourself - are they really about Cromwell? A little reflection should suggest to you that the answer is that they are not. The technique being used by the examiner here is the familiar one of throwing light on a period by referring to what had gone before. You are being asked to assess the character of the years 1658-60 by contrasting it with the relative stability of the preceding period. Of course, you need knowledge of that earlier time (consult Chapters 3 and 7) to make the comparison, but the focus is on the period 1658-60.

An effective approach to question 7 might be along the following lines. From your notes draw up a list of the weaknesses of the republican cause; these might include lack of unity among the political and military republicans (Haselrig and Lambert illustrate this point well), their failure to seize their opportunities earlier in the 1658-59 period, and their military weakness as shown by Lambert's inability to challenge Monk. It would be appropriate then to describe the growing strength of the monarchical reaction by May 1660; Monk is obviously important here, as is the broad movement towards a return to the original constitution among all but the radicals, who were a dwindling influence by 1660. A key point to emphasise is that by May 1660, republicanism was largely discredited. It was perceived to have had 11 years in which to find the answers to the nation's problems and to have failed. As the response to Charles II's Declaration of Breda showed, monarchy was deemed to have far more to offer in 1660.

Source-based questions on 'The Path to Restoration, 1658-60'

1 The Challenge to Army Rule
Study the French Ambassador's description on pages 96-7 and the three petitions on pages 97-8. Answer the following questions:
a) What picture of the unrest in London can be drawn from the French Ambassador's description? (6 marks)
b) How far do the three petitions express a common set of grievances? (7 marks)
c) How useful is this collection of sources to the historian who is seeking to understand the reasons for the recall of the Rump in December 1659? (8 marks)
d) To what extent does the evidence in these sources suggest that the collapse of the republic was imminent? (9 marks)

2 Monk and the Restoration

Study Monk's declaration on page 96, Charles II's letter on page 100 and the Declaration of Breda on page 101. Answer the following questions:

a) Using your own knowledge and the evidence in Monk's declaration and the king's letter, examine the motives that led Monk to march into England in January 1660. (7 marks)

b) Analyse the significance of the following terms as they appear in the Declaration of Breda: 'liberty to tender consciences' (lines 9-10, page 101). (3 marks) 'all arrears due to the officers and soldiers' (line 21, page 101). (3 marks)

c) How far does your reading of the evidence support the contention that the Declaration of Breda 'revealed an astute perception of the outstanding grievances of the time'? (8 marks)

d) Drawing on your own knowledge and the evidence in these sources, comment on the assertion that the Restoration owed less to Monk's action than to Charles II's inaction. (9 marks)

CHAPTER 7

Conclusion: The Interregnum in Perspective

Some modern scholars argue that the real significance of the Interregnum lies in what it discredited. Others see it less negatively and suggest that in many respects it was a time of major achievement. But whatever line they take, historians agree in regarding the Interregnum as an extraordinary period whose mixture of reaction and experimentation demands analysis. This chapter offers a series of key points in that analysis as a way of providing the reader with a framework for assessing the character and importance of the 11 years without a king.

The Restoration settlement that followed the accession of Charles II in 1660 attempted to expunge all that had happened since 1649, thereby suggesting that the Interregnum had been an aberration. The execution of the surviving regicides and the grisly disinterring and public hanging of Oliver Cromwell's body were intended to symbolise the obliteration of an unworthy period of history. This was how the royalist commentators and chroniclers wished it to be. But too much had happened during the Interregnum for it simply to be dismissed as an unhappy memory.

Although monarchy was restored it was not a complete restoration of former royal power. Christopher Hill has pointed out memorably that after the events of 1649 English monarchs 'never forgot that they had a joint in their neck', meaning that royal absolutism was now no longer possible. 1660 was as much a restoration of parliament as of monarchy. Charles II was always aware of this and was careful never to push his differences with parliament too far. When his brother James II (1685-8) ignored the lessons of the Interregnum and tried to reimpose royal absolutism he lost his throne. 'The Glorious Revolution' of 1689 which saw William III accept the Crown on the terms laid down by parliament was the certain end of any notion of absolute monarchy.

The Interregnum also established the place of parliament as a central and necessary part of the constitution. This may appear an odd claim in view of the chequered history of parliament during those years. The forcible expulsion of the Rump in 1653, the contempt in which the Nominated Assembly came to be held, and the unhappy relations of the two Protectors with their parliaments, none of which ran their full term, hardly suggest that it was a time of success. But the notable thing is how persistent Cromwell was in his belief that parliament was an essential institution. He may have declared that all constitutional forms were 'but dung and dross in comparison of Christ', but he never wholly abandoned the attempt to find one that worked. This was because he accepted that the only alternative to parliament was unfettered military rule. It is also highly significant that it was parliament that invited

Charles to return to the throne in 1660. In doing this it gave practical expression to the theory that henceforward parliament's relations with monarchy would be a matter of partnership rather than subservience.

The fundamental flaw in all the governments of the Interregnum was that their authority rested on a seizure of power, in the form of Pride's Purge and the execution of the reigning monarch. Thereafter, none of them could claim to rule by consent; all of them were imposed. Scarcely 10 per cent of MPs had accepted parliament's right to put Charles I on trial. Moreover, modern estimates suggest that none of the regimes that held office between 1649 and 1660 had the genuine support of more than one in ten of the population. Consequently, they governed solely in terms of their own asserted authority. They could not legitimately claim to represent the nation. The break with tradition implicit in the abolition of monarchy meant that they could not ground their authority in precedent.

This would not have mattered had any of the regimes of the Interregnum been genuinely revolutionary. But the persistent argument of the Commonwealth and Protectorate governments was that their rule was in keeping with 'the ancient constitution'. Indeed, they repeatedly claimed that they were restoring the fundamental laws and liberties of the nation. But this claim was undermined by the reality of the situation. Events between 1649 and 1660 showed that Britain never became fully reconciled to military rule. It is clear that the traditional propertied classes wanted a return to civilian authority. The localities were unhappy with the attempts at centralising that occurred in the 1650s. This was most evident in the unpopularity of the Major-Generals and in local resistance to the idea of centrally imposed taxation; the 'decimation' tax and the 'assessments', raised to maintain the army, were particularly resented.

The experience of the 1650s gave England a strong distaste for standing armies. None of the governments of the Commonwealth and Protectorate was able to make itself independent of the military. Oliver Cromwell aimed to return England to secure and stable civil government, but the paradox was that to achieve this he had to use the only means at his disposal, which were military. He had perforce to employ the very system he was endeavouring to abandon. That was one of the reasons why he gave serious thought to the offer of monarchy in 1657; kingship would have enabled him to detach himself constitutionally from reliance on the army. It was also the case that by 1659 General George Monk, the architect of the restoration, had come to believe that the only effective way in which military rule could be ended was by a return to traditional monarchy, the system under which the executive authority was independent of army control.

Military regimes are invariably highly expensive and it was in regard to finance that the governments of the Interregnum were at their weakest. The civil wars between king and parliament had been in part a consequence of the dispute over the right of the monarch to impose financial levies on his subjects. It was, therefore, ironic that the Commonwealth and Protectorate governments should have had to resort to techniques of raising revenue that were even more severe than those the Long Parliament had protested against before 1642. The insuperable difficulty for the Rump and for the Protectorate was that the available revenue was inadequate to meet their needs. They were faced with the double problem that the various revenue expedients failed to raise sufficient money while at the same time making the governments who tried to impose them highly unpopular.

If finance proved an insoluble difficulty during the Interregnum, so, too, did religion. The failures of the various Protectorate parliaments to carry the nation towards godly rule and the fear that the wilder sectaries inspired in the hearts of moderates and traditionalists in this period combined to further the notion that religion was necessarily a disruptive force when applied to politics. The Interregnum destroyed the idea of England's ever being a confessional or theocratic state. Religion would certainly remain a major factor in British politics after the Restoration, but no serious attempt would again be made to base government purely on religious principles.

Whatever the weaknesses internally, there is little doubt that England experienced one of her most notable periods as an international power during the Interregnum. Her military might, the extension of her overseas territories and the defeat of Holland and Spain were extraordinary triumphs. In addition, the Protectorate period was one of considerable commercial expansion. In some respects this was a by-product of the various wars in which England engaged. Although these wars were presented as religious crusades, the effect of the defeat of the Dutch and the Spanish was to secure England's control of the seas, giving her merchants access to all the disputed trading regions in the known world. The same expansion occurred in colonial affairs. Indeed, many historians regard this period as marking the beginning of Britain as an Empire.

The Interregnum was, therefore, more than simply a break in the continuity of traditional kingship, and it would be unhistorical to regard the period only in negative terms. Important advances were made in key areas of administration: finance, law and local government all underwent significant modification and development. Despite the apparent failure of the rule of the Major-Generals, relations and communications between London and the provinces were made smoother. In this context care needs to be taken not to overstate the degree of central authority applied in these years. Central government lacked the bureaucratic machinery to enforce its will. It was always dependent upon the co-operation of the traditional ruling authorities in the localities. Moreover the evidence drawn from the wide research into local history reveals how great was the continuity of magistrates and JPs in the local community. It was never Cromwell's intention to usurp what he regarded as the 'natural' authority of the local governing classes. Indeed, his aim was to forge a harmony of interest between the Protectorate and the community. In this he again showed his basic social conservatism.

Oliver Cromwell was, of course, the dominant figure of the period. If there is one thing that his career during the Interregnum illustrates it is that good intentions are not enough. His hope that after the traumas of the civil wars the nation would adopt godly government and abandon discord proved unrealistic. Religious bitterness and political strife did not end with the execution of the king; they became even more intense.

There has long been a major historiographical debate over whether the years 1640-60 constituted a revolution. Indeed, a leading contributor to that debate, Gerald Aylmer, entitles one of his books *Rebellion or Revolution?*. What can be said is that even if the years from 1640-49 are interpreted as a revolution, since they involved a successful challenge to traditional monarchy that culminated in the execution of the reigning king, the following 11 years did not consolidate that revolution. Notwithstanding the excitement and fears created by the religious sectaries and political radicals, the predominant feature of the time was the strength and persistence of conservative attitudes. Few of those in positions of real influence after 1649 wanted to challenge the existing social order. Their criterion for judging the worth of the constitutional experiments that were introduced during the Interregnum was how well they preserved and protected the established order from social and religious disruption. There is little doubt that the political and religious radicalism of the times frightened the nobility and gentry and made them determined to resist the extension of rights to the lower orders. Thus, the events of the Interregnum, far from encouraging social revolution, made the conservative classes more conservative still. John Morrill summarises the impact in these terms:

1 The English Revolution consolidated the elite when it might have destroyed it; consolidated order by giving everyone a taste of, and distaste for, disorder; prepared the way for the collapse of the confessional State while discrediting the Puritan dream of a godly
5 commonwealth.

However, this reversion to conservatism does not in itself prove that the Restoration was inevitable. Monarchy was not necessarily seen as the guarantee of order; the image of Charles I as 'that man of blood', responsible for bringing about the civil wars, was still a potent one. Had the Commonwealth or Protectorate been able to offer genuine hope of a satisfactory and lasting civil settlement, the established classes may well have found them acceptable. But the truth was that Cromwell was never able to transform his military authority into a genuinely civilian one.

After his death the struggle for power within the military and among the political factions convinced all those with a vested interest in preserving order and stability that there really was no alternative to a return to the pre-1649 condition of things, this time with a king who would respect the limits of his power.

The period was extraordinarily rich in the outpouring of political and religious ideas. It was perhaps too rich. Mixed in with intense belief was a great deal of confusion of thought and ambiguity of attitude. It is difficult to avoid the conclusion that even in an age of religious fervour, such as the period 1640-60 was, feelings of self-interest and self-protection predominated. People seldom act out of pure principle or abstract belief. When extreme political activists or rabid religious sectaries threatened the existing social order people were willing to see Cromwell as a guardian, but when the army demanded heavy taxation and enforced billeting of soldiers they just as readily saw him as an oppressor. Behind the talk of constitutions and settlements was a deep concern to gain or retain position and privilege. This was hardly the stuff of revolution. The notion of society as a hierarchical order was far too deeply entrenched for it to be seriously threatened by the political or religious radicals.

Using the 'Conclusion'

This chapter offers three main conclusions:

1   The importance of the Interregnum lies essentially in its negative aspects. The events of the years 1649-60 discredited a number of notions in regard to monarchy, parliament, government, army, religion, and finance.
2   There are, nevertheless, certain positive features which should not be overlooked. Outstanding among these are foreign affairs.
3   The Interregnum rather than being a revolutionary period marked a retreat from revolution.

It would help you to ensure that you have acquired an effective over-view of the topic if you were to test the validity of these three propositions by measuring them against the notes you made on the earlier chapters of the book, and by asking yourself how far they accord with the viewpoints of the other writers whose work you have studied on this period.

1649-60 - the questions:

a period of experiment?	a period of failure?
a period of achievement?	a retreat from revolution?

the considerations:

monarchy • parliament • government • army • foreign affairs • religion • finance

Summary - The Interregnum in Perspective

Chronological Table

1648	Dec	Pride's Purge
1649	Jan	trial and execution of Charles I
		the Commons claimed 'supreme power'
	Feb	Charles II proclaimed King in Scotland
		Council of State appointed
	Mar	Rump abolished Monarchy and Lords
		Cromwell appointed Lord Lieutenant in charge of parliament's army
	Apr	Digger commune set up in Surrey
	May	England declared to be a Commonwealth
		Leveller rising against Rump crushed by Cromwell
	Aug	Cromwell lands in Ireland
	Sept	Siege of Drogheda
	Oct	Siege of Wexford
1650	Jan	Engagement Act
	May	Rump recalled Cromwell to England
	June	Cromwell replaced Fairfax as Commander-in-Chief
	July	Treason Act
	Aug	Blasphemy Act
		Cromwell entered Scotland
	Sept	Cromwell's victory over Scots at Dunbar
1651	Jan	Charles II crowned in Scotland
	Sept	Cromwell defeated Charles II at Worcester
	Oct	Navigation Act introduced
		Charles II escaped to France
1652	May	outbreak of the Dutch War
	July	Fleetwood became Commander-in-Chief in Ireland
	Aug	Settlement of Ireland Act began the Cromwellian land confiscations
		Committee for the Propagation of the Gospel formed
1653	Apr	Cromwell dispersed the Rump
	Jul–Dec	Nominated Assembly
	July	new Council of State appointed by Assembly
	Aug	Tromp killed in the defeat of the Dutch off Texel
	Dec	Nominated Assembly dissolved itself
		Instrument of Government adopted
		Cromwell installed as Lord Protector
1654	Apr	Dutch War ended
		Treaty with Sweden
		Act of Union with Scotland
	July	Treaty with Portugal
	Sept	first parliament of Protectorate
		Treaty with Denmark

	Dec	English fleet sailed against Spanish colonies
1655	Jan	Cromwell dissolved first Protectorate parliament
	Mar	Penruddock's rising
	May	English forces failed to take Hispaniola
		English capture of Jamaica
	Oct	beginning of rule of Major-Generals
		defensive alliance with France
1656	Sept	second Protectorate parliament
		beginning of war with Spain
		parliament's prosecution of James Nayler
1657	Jan	parliament declined to renew Decimation Tax
		abandonment of Major-Generals
	Feb	Cromwell offered the kingship
	Mar	military agreement with France
	Apr	Cromwell declined kingship
	May	*Humble Petition and Advice* accepted by Cromwell
	July	first session of parliament
	Oct	capture of Mardyke
1658	Jan-Feb	second session of parliament
	Feb	Cromwell dissolved parliament
	June	Battle of the Dunes
		England acquired Dunkirk
	Sept	death of Oliver Cromwell
		Richard Cromwell became Protector
1659	Jan-Apr	third Protectorate parliament
	Apr	Richard Cromwell resigned - end of the Protectorate
	May	the Commonwealth restored - Rump re-assembled
		end of Spanish war
	Aug	Booth's Rising
	Oct	army expelled the Rump
	Oct-Dec	government by Committee of Safety
		widespread disturbances throughout England
	Dec	Rump re-assembled
1660	Jan	Monk's troops crossed from Scotland to England
	Feb	Monk's troops reached London
		return of excluded members to the Rump
		Rump dissolved
	Mar	Long Parliament restored
	Apr-May	Convention Parliament
	Apr	Lambert's army defeated at Edgehill
		House of Lords re-convened
		Charles II issued Declaration of Breda
		both Houses voted to accept Declaration of Breda
	May 8	Charles II proclaimed king
	May 29	Charles II entered London

Glossary

Anti-Christ   a Calvinist term applied to the damned and their behaviour

Arminianism   a doctrine that rejected predestination and taught that salvation came via God's sanctifying grace as dispensed through the sacraments of the church

assessment   a parliamentary tax levied monthly on land and property

Calvinism   a strict form of Protestantism, deriving from the teachings of Jean Calvin (1509-64) and characterised by a belief in predestination

Covenanters   Scottish Presbyterians who swore by the Solemn League and Covenant to introduce their form of worship as the state religion in England. They were the main supporters of Charles II in Scotland, 1649-51

decimation   a tax imposed during the Interregnum on known royalists

Diggers   the mocking title for the 'true levellers', who called for an end of private property and set up idealistic communes in the 1650s in the belief that land belonged not to individuals but to the community

elect   the Calvinist term for those predestined for salvation

Engagers   Scottish Presbyterians who took an 'Engagement' to press for the establishment of Presbyterianism as the state religion in England. Both Charles I and Charles II entered into agreements with them

episopacy   the governing bishops within a church system

godly   as a noun, it referred to those predestined for salvation (alternative terms are the 'saints' or the 'elect')

Grandees   the officers who belonged to the Council of the Army

indemnity   the guarantee of protection against prosecution for acts committed during the civil wars - consistently demanded by the troops throughout the Interregnum

Independents   the Protestant separatist sects that refused to recognise the authority of a state church whether Anglican or Presbyterian

Jesuits   the Society of Jesus, a special order of priests set up in 1540 and dedicated to defending the Roman Catholic Church against the forces of Protestantism

Laudianism	the English form of Arminianism that took its name from Archbishop Laud, who emphasised the need for conformity of worship and obedience
Levellers	a radical urban movement of the 1640s that claimed that sovereignty lay not with governments but with the people
Mass	the central Roman Catholic ritual, involving the act of consecration at which, believers held, the sacramental bread and wine turned into the real body and blood of Christ (transubstantiation)
mercantilism	a form of trade warfare based on protectionism
millenarianism	the belief that the known world was about to end and the 1000-year reign of Christ and His saints begin
Popery	an abusive Puritan term to describe Roman Catholicism
Prayer Book	the Laudian church manual, which laid down detailed regulations about the way in which public worship was to be conducted
predestination	the Calvinist belief that denied free will and held that individuals were either saved or damned from the moment of conception
prerogative	the monarch's royal power which stood outside the jurisdiction of the common law
Presbyterianism	was of two distinct varieties: the dogmatic Scottish form with its belief in a strongly-centralised church organised by elders, and the milder English form, sometimes known as political presbyterianism, whose main idea was of a church without bishops
Puritanism	has no precise denominational meaning; it is generally used to refer to the stricter forms of Protestant belief
radicalism	the belief that society must be not merely reformed but changed at its roots
regicides	those who signed the death warrant of Charles I
thorough	the policy of strong central government, associated with Strafford in the 1630s
tithe	tax levied locally for the upkeep of ministers of the parish church
triers and ejectors	a body of Commissioners, set up by Cromwell in 1653, charged with the responsibility of selecting and supervising the ministers of the church

Further Reading

There is now a wealth of excellent books on the Interregnum. The following is a very selective list of works which will be of particular interest to the student.

Outstandingly-good introductory surveys are:

Toby Barnard, *The English Republic 1649-60* (Longman 1982). This is a short but still comprehensive survey, with a good selection of sources.

Austin Woolrych, *England Without a King* (Methuen 1983). This is an even briefer study, but a masterful analysis by one of the acknowledged authorities on the period. Many of the author's observations on the earlier part of the Interregnum are developed in detail in his *Commonwealth to Protectorate* (OUP 1983)

John Morrill (Editor), *Revolution and Restoration: England in the 1650s* (Collins and Brown 1992). This is a collection of seven essays containing some of the latest researches on the period.

Ronald Hutton, *The British Republic, 1649-60* (Macmillan 1990). Hutton is a provocative writer, concerned here with stressing that the Interregnum should be seen in a British not just an English context.

Gerald Aylmer, *Rebellion or Revolution* (OUP 1986). This takes 1640 as its starting point and, therefore, covers a wider area. Written by one of the leading scholars on Stuart history, this has become a standard text. It complements an earlier collection of essays which Aylmer edited: *The Interregnum: the Quest for Settlement* (1972)

Among the broader treatments of the period to be recommended are:

John Kenyon, *The Stuart Constitution* (CUP, second edition 1986). This book has established itself as an essential source-study of the period.

Derek Hirst, *Authority and Conflict: England 1603-60* (Edward Arnold 1986). An important revisionist look at the period; this is well worth comparing with:

Christopher Hill, *The Century of Revolution, 1603-1714* (Nelson 1961). This is just one of the very many works by the most prolific writer on the period. Hill has modified his own views since writing this, but it remains an interesting example of the determinist approach.

Conrad Russell, *The Crisis of Parliaments: English History 1509-1660* (OUP 1971). The later chapters of this book will introduce the student to some of the key ideas of one of the leading contributors to the analysis of the English Revolution.

Samuel Gardiner, *History of the Commonwealth and Protectorate* (Longman 1903). Although written about a century ago, these volumes are still revered by modern scholars for their combination of scholarship and flowing narrative. It would be a pity if students denied themselves the pleasure of such a good read.

There will doubtless never be complete agreement about the character and achievements of Oliver Cromwell, the dominant figure of the Interregnum. Of the many modern studies the following are recommended:

Barry Coward, *Oliver Cromwell* (Longman 1991). This is the most up-to-date, balanced, and perhaps the most accessible modern biography of Cromwell. This should be compared with:

Christopher Hill, *God's Englishman: Oliver Cromwell and the English Revolution* (1970). This is an interpretation of Cromwell as religious zealot and bourgeois revolutionary.

Ivan Roots, (Editor) *Cromwell a Profile* (Macmillan 1973). This is an important collection of essays by major Cromwellian experts.

John Morrill (Editor) *Oliver Cromwell and the English Revolution* (Longman 1990). This gathers together some of the most recent reappraisals of the Protector.

Three biographies which give interesting and contrasting perspectives on Cromwell are:
Pauline Gregg, *Oliver Cromwell* (Dent 1988);
Antonia Fraser, *Cromwell: Our Chief of Men* (Weidenfeld and Nicholson 1973); and
Veronica Wedgwood, *Oliver Cromwell* (1964).

The radical movements of the period are covered in:
Christopher Hill, *The World Turned Upside Down* (Penguin 1975);
Frances Dow, *Radicalism in the English Revolution 1640-1660,* (Blackwell 1985);
Robert Acheson, *Radical Puritans in England 1550-1660* (Longman 1990)

Index

Argyll, Marquess of 28

Barkstead, John 44

Berry, James 44

Bethel, Slingsby 81, 87

Blake, Robert 76

Booth, Sir George 95, 102, 104

Broghill, Lord 49

Butler, William 45

Charles I 1-10, 17, 22, 23, 28, 30,
    33-5, 54, 60, 63, 74-6, 88, 89, 91,
    93, 99, 110, 112

Charles II 1, 23, 29, 66, 95, 100, 101,
    102, 104, 105, 106, 107, 108,
    109, 110

Charles X 81, 85

Clarendon, Earl of 12, 87, 101

Clarkson, Laurence 59

Crawford, Major-General 63

Cromwell, Oliver 5-7, 9-21, 24-7, 29,
    30, 37-44, 46-58, 60-5, 67-73,
    75, 77, 78, 81, 83-7, 89-91,
    102-4, 106, 109, 110, 112, 113

Cromwell, Richard 10, 85, 91, 92, 93,
    94, 105

Desborough, John 45, 49, 92, 98, 100

De Witt, John 76

Elizabeth I 31, 67, 74, 85

Essex, Earl of 5

Everard, William 22

Fairfax, Lady 8

Fairfax, Thomas 7, 15, 16, 19, 22, 29

Fleetwood, Charles 27, 45, 92, 93, 98,
    100

Fox, George 62, 63

Gough, William 45, 46, 92

Harrison, Thomas 16, 34, 39, 40, 60,
    61

Haselrig, Arthur 53, 95, 99, 100, 107

Henrietta Maria 4

Henry VIII 74

Ireton, Henry 16, 20, 27

James I 74

James II 109

Kelsey, Thomas 45, 46

Lambert, John 29, 34, 39-42, 44, 45,
    53, 79, 95, 96, 98, 99, 100, 103,
    107

Laud, William 2, 4, 6, 14, 31

Lenthall, William 50

Leslie, David 29

Lilburne, John 18, 19, 20, 21, 37

Ludlow, Edmund 51

Manchester, Earl of 5

Marten, Henry 20

Marvell, Andrew 87

Mazarin, Cardinal 83

Monk, George 29, 49, 92, 96-101,
    103-6, 107, 108, 110

Montague, Edward 99

Montrose, Earl of 28

Muggleton, Lodowick 61

Nayler, James 49, 62, 63, 65

O'Neill, Owen Roe 24, 25

Ormonde, Earl of 23, 24, 25

Overton, Richard 20

Packer, William 45, 63, 72

Penn, William 79

Penruddock, John 45, 67, 68, 70, 71,
    72

Pepys, Samuel 68, 87

Pride, Colonel 7, 15

Pym, John 3

Skippon, Philip 45

St. John, Oliver 76

Strafford, Earl of 2, 3, 4, 14, 23

Thurloe, John 67, 68

Van Tromp, Admiral 76

Vane, Henry 81

Venables, Robert 79

Venner, Thomas 61

Wallington, Nehemiah 23

Walsingham, Francis 67

Walwyn, William 20

Whalley, Edward 45, 46, 92

Whitelocke, Bulstrode 50

William I 32

William III 109

Worsley, Charles 45, 46